THE RHETORIC OF THE
CONTEMPORARY LYRIC

THE RHETORIC OF THE CONTEMPORARY LYRIC

BY

JONATHAN HOLDEN

 Indiana University Press • *Bloomington*

Manufactured in the United States of America

Library of Congress Cataloging in Publication Data
Holden, Jonathan.
The rhetoric of the contemporary lyric.

1. American poetry—20th century—History and
criticism—Addresses, essays, lectures.   2. Poetics—
Addresses, essays, lectures.   I. Title.
PS323.5H56   1980   811'.54'09   79-3383
ISBN 0-253-15667-X   1   2   3   4   5   84   83   82   81   80

For my parents

CONTENTS

INTRODUCTION

The following seven essays, as they emerged over a span of about three years, were conceived independently of each other. Each was prompted by what appeared at the time to be a discrete issue, a particular occasion. In the earliest of these essays, "Syntax and the Poetry of John Ashbery," I first began to clarify in my own mind a growing conviction that most well-made poems exhibit a pronounced syntax, not simply within the interval of a sentence, but over longer intervals; that in many of my favorite poems this "syntax" is like the best prose syntax in miniature; that the shape of a good poem is in fact often like that of a single sentence. I had noticed that, when I was writing poetry, the discovery that would allow me suddenly to move ahead and to find a shape to a poem was often syntactical: perhaps some form of parallel structure; perhaps a narrative format suggested by a factor as seemingly minor as a choice of tense; perhaps the discovery that the most appropriate "grammar" for a given poem consisted of a list of sentence fragments; or perhaps the imitation of some already familiar grammar, for example, the instructional format described in the essay "The 'Found' in Contemporary Poetry." In the Ashbery essay, as I tried to isolate the kinds of syntax that I find beautiful, I hit upon the admittedly gimmicky device of rewriting a prose paragraph by D. H. Lawrence, of preserving its syntax but changing its sense. Although not a very rigorous or orthodox way of approaching the issue of syntax in a poem, the exercise had the virtue of providing very concrete examples of the principle I was trying to make clear—examples that are, if not conclusive, at least evocative and fun to compare to one another. I regarded the hypothetical revisions almost as laboratory experiments, as an inductive method by which some principles of literature could be empirically tested and, in a sense, verified, though no such thing as a "proof" has existed or ever will exist in the domain of literature.

The method of offering playfully serious revisions of a text in order to reveal some of its elements or to illustrate some abstract principle was so exhilarating and afforded me such a feeling of leverage that, when I contemplated the second essay, "'Affected Naturalness' and the Poetry of Sensibility," I was drawn to the method again. In fact, the whole essay is built around rewritings. I had, for some time, wondered if one could take a good poem in an outmoded style and, by rewriting it in a fashionable style, make it acceptable again. The essay that resulted is nothing more than a demonstration of how one might go about trying to do this, and the conclusions I drew from my own attempts.

The third in the order that these essays were written is "'The Found' in Contemporary Poetry." Like that of the Ashbery essay, its real occasion was my attempt to work through problems and doubts I was having with my own writing of poems. As in both the Ashbery essay and "'Affected Naturalness,'" I used the gimmick of rewriting in order to try to put, in the most concrete terms possible, the question that was bothering me, one that still bothers me sometimes: Why write in verse? Naive as it may sound, I have always assumed that each medium—painting, music, photography, literature, cinema, live drama, and so on—is ideally adapted to perform certain tasks better than any of the others, that each has a kind of *raison d'être* that is somehow functional. Far better, for example, to try to render color in paint than in words. An epic battle scene is, I like to think, better presented on a wide screen than on a live stage. Similarly, I would argue that literature is the medium and that the novel is the genre best adapted to explore and to render the inner life of characters and to portray the complexity of an individual personality; internal monologue and the mention of characters' thoughts and feelings is so much more fluently handled in literary narration than in, say, cinema, which has its own unique potentiality. In short, though I have never tested this belief, I have always envisioned what a colleague once called, when I mentioned my theory to her, a kind of "ecology" among the arts. As an example of the way in which the ironclad laws of this ecology function, I suspect that the invention of photography has had something to do with the drift in painting toward the figurative and that cinema has similarly influenced both live drama and prose fiction.

Within the domain of literature, I have found it convenient to assume that there must be a similar ecology, that genres ultimately have some functional basis that, like the evolution of folk medicine, has tended over the years to shape their conventions. Thus, when I am writing poetry, the question What is poetry? tends to present itself in practical terms: Would this material be better in a short story or in a novel, or is it best in verse? This question is, I guess, just a rephrased version of the question as to whether there is any "essential difference between the language of prose and metrical composition"—an issue that has been with us at least as long as Wordsworth's "Preface"—but at no time has the issue been more troubling, it seems to me, than it is now, especially with the normalization of free verse, the widespread popularity of the prose poem, and the proliferation of an extremely colloquial diction in most American poetry.

The question of why I am putting *this* into *verse* is one I routinely ask and sometimes agonize over when I struggle with a poem. I find this question unavoidable. "'The Found' in Contemporary Poetry" is my attempt to tackle the question in the crudest and most obvious way I could think of. Using the method of rewriting, which I was beginning to believe in, I selected certain texts and compared my response to each when it was set in prose with my response to it when it was set in verse. What I learned from these comparisons seems to be that we tend to read a text far differently when it is in verse than when it is in prose, that verse is itself a "convention" that profoundly directs a reader's expectations, and that, particularly now, with the gradual recession of rhyme, meter, and other orthodox poetic conventions in favor of our current, open-form poetry, almost the only clear advantage left to verse is its capacity to allude to the dormant conventions without actually reproducing them. I was struck with the extent to which expectations generated by a verse or a prose format are being artfully exploited by some of our poets—in particular, Stephen Dunn—and I began to wonder whether, in such a queasy, unstructured poetic climate as obtains right now, the choice of verse over prose proceeds more from rhetorical than from structural considerations. This is why, in the remainder of the essays, the theme of the "rhetoric" of the contemporary lyric recurs so frequently.

Although I am quite aware that the term "rhetoric" no longer refers to the art of oratory but refers more to "style," I still tend to regard rhetoric as having something to do with persuasion; and, unfashionable as it may seem, I have used it in roughly this way throughout these essays. To be specific: If "rhetoric" is traditionally the "art of persuasion," then, whenever we consider the ways in which a poet or novelist might have tried to anticipate and play upon the expectations and the disposition of his audience, we are considering the rhetorical aspects of a work of imaginative literature. To narrow my usage further: Throughout these essays the rhetorical aspects of a poem or any piece of literature are those that touch on the issue of *who is speaking to whom, through what mask, and for what ostensible purpose.*

Questions of style are, of course, related to the definition above, but I see style as a secondary consideration, dependent on mask. For example, a college teacher might be faced, in his opening lecture, with the question of what kind of image he wanted the class to have of him.[1] Should the class look up to him as some infallible gray eminence? Or should he minimize the threshold separating himself from the students, admit his own doubts and limitations, treat his students as friends rather than as pupils. Clearly, although the style of his delivery to the opening class—his diction, his body language, even his dress—could, in a loose sense of that term, be construed as his "rhetoric," such a rhetoric will, if analyzed, be seen to proceed from a more fundamental strategy, from a premeditated answer to the question of who is speaking to whom, through what mask, and for what ostensible purpose.

The way in which style may be construed as secondary to rhetoric, as I define rhetoric, is perhaps better appreciated in the domain of literature. When a poet chooses to write a sonnet, his stylistic possibilities are almost sure to be circumscribed. In part because the convention calls for rhymes and a metric, the style of the sonnet is apt to be relatively formal and literary. Because the rhyme scheme is a frame inviting blocks of an argument and a resolution to it, the movement of the poem is apt to be logical, dialectical; and this movement, like the movement of a debate, will enforce its own stylistic decorum. In open-form poetry, simply the choice of, say, the first-person-singular pronoun as the governing pronoun of a poem is a fundamental rhetorical decision—the decision to pretend to go naked—that will constrain the poet to adopt a style appropriate to that mask, which is a kind of contract—the set of expectations set up by "I"—established with the reader. The rhetorical disposition of a poem, then, is its stance, which may be efficiently reinforced by an appropriate style or be subverted by an inappropriate style. Deployment of "I" is not part of a style: it is a convention that requires a style.

The fourth in the order that these essays were written is "The Abuse of the Second-Person Pronoun." The essay examines precisely the issue of pronouns that I have raised above, and it tries to demonstrate, through the technique of rewriting, how the "rhetorical disposition" of certain poems can be muddied by improper choice of a governing pronoun, particularly the fashionable "blurred-you." The essay rather rashly hints at authorial intentionality because, for reasons that are almost self-evident, it is almost impossible to analyze the rhetorical aspect of a poem (by my definition) without seeming to commit the "intentional fallacy." In my defense I would like to point out, however, that, whereas the intentional fallacy is associated with a poetry ready-made for the New Criticism—a poetry that, even more than the great modernist poems of Eliot and Pound, carried to an extreme the dogma that good poetry necessitates "extinction of the personality"—in any consideration of the more personalized poetry that succeeded the New-Critical mode, the intentional fallacy is of doubtful value. The more a poem resembles personal testimony, the more its effectiveness is going to hinge on the reader's judgment of the poem's sincerity. Yet to render a verbal judgment about a poem's sincerity is, in a sense, to commit the fallacy. For example, it is impossible to decide how to take a poem such as Sylvia Plath's "Daddy" without also making a decision— admittedly a guess—about what her intention was: Is the poem intended as "light verse"? How much self-mockery is in its tone? Does one hear anguish or rage or mostly ghoulish humor? One circles the poem, testing it, guessing, listening for a crack in the voice or a cackle. But, when one finally renders a judgment on an issue like this, no matter how tactfully one phrases it, one commits the fallacy because the very nature of "sincerity" is such that, no matter how uncategorical the language in which a judgment is couched may sound, one has to commit oneself to a categorical judgment about an author's intention. When a critic says something like "Poem X is moving, it has the ring of sincerity—the anguish of personal testimony," he is trying to say, "Poem X may not be sincere, but it sounds sincere—sincere enough to be moving." The trouble is that we are never moved by testimony unless we believe that it *is* sincere. Frankly, I do not see how one can read any text and be sensitive to the conventions on which it rests without making a plethora of assumptions about the author's intentions, without listening for a human voice behind the printed page, and without taking that voice seriously, letting oneself be led by it. Consider the pun on "mourning" in the beginning of John Crowe Ransom's great poem, "Janet Waking": "Beautifully Janet slept/ Till it was deeply morning. . . ." If the pun is "unintentional," then the tone of the first line—a cue to the complex tone of the rest of the poem—is rather more lugubrious than any staunch advocate of the intentional fallacy has suspected. To decide on tone—that is, to respond to it— is to decide on authorial intention. I think that too often the intentional fallacy seduces us into treating a poem as some precious linguistic game that can be divorced wholly from life, when, in fact, poetry is a human art that springs straight from the blood and mire of a person's existence. What value the intentional fallacy has is to remind us of truths so obvious that they are trivial: belief and certainty are not to be confused; we can never be certain of an author's intentions without asking the author; a work of art is liable to be far more complex and ambivalent than could be accounted for in terms of the author's conscious intentions.

To approach a poem as a piece of rhetoric, as I have defined that word, is time and again to allude to an author's intentions. For example, to ask what effect a different title would have on a given poem is to ask what the author's intentions were in choosing this wording instead of that wording. To ask what the effect would be if the pronoun "he" were substituted for "I" throughout a given poem is, likewise, to inquire implicitly as to the author's intentions, because the choice of a pronoun for a poem is such a fundamental, tactical decision that, whether made intuitively or through logical deliberation, it is a choice probably any good poet is conscious of having made and can rationalize. For example, to say the line of verse "I drift out to the darkening evening" is to pretend to be talking to oneself, reliving some emotional process aloud, unconscious of being overheard by the audience. If we substitute "he" for "I" so that version two reads "He drifts out to the darkening evening," no longer is the speaker musing to himself. Instead, he is pretending to address the reader directly in order to narrate a story in the third person. Suppose we translate the original line without a pronoun change into the past tense so that version three reads "I drifted out to the darkening evening." Again, the poem has become narrative; the speaker's perspective on the events and feelings he is relating is enlarged because he has the advantage of hindsight. Each of these pronoun choices constitutes a different rhetorical contract. Who is addressing whom, through what mask, and for what ostensible purpose—the format of the contract consists of four basic terms, and, in versions two and three, three of the four terms are rewritten. In version one the poet is talking to himself in the pressure of the moment, unaware that he is being overheard, spontaneously impelled into a burst of solitary song. In version two the poet is talking directly to his audience, his text is somewhat more premeditated than in version one, the story is a mask or a metaphor for some personal concern of the speaker, whose empathy for the "he" (the poem's protagonist) is augmented by the present tense. The ostensible purpose of the text is to tell a story with some point to it. In version three the poet is talking directly to the audience, and the narrative is premeditated. The speaker's perspective on events is particularly broad, because eventually the story will tell how the speaker transcended some experience; hence the act of narration involves a kind of transcendence "about" (of) transcendence. The story is thus a mask for the poet's sense of growth and transcendence rather than for any lesson suggested by the narrated events themselves, and the ostensible purpose of the poem is not strictly narrative but is to appeal directly to the reader to compare the reader's own experience to that of the speaker. Each of these contracts involves such fundamental considerations that it is impossible to imagine a poet's not asking, at some point of the composition, questions such as Do I want this poem in the present tense? and Do I want it in the first person? The less poetry makes use of orthodox conventions, which, as Eliot saw, tend to depersonalize poetry by fusing the poet's voice with the medley of voices that make up The Tradition, the more a poet, alone somewhere, launching his tentative song, is going to be beset with choices involving the rhetoric of his stance, his situation. And, whenever somebody reads a poem, the more he or she is going to wonder, Was this meant for me? How does it touch my life?

The remaining three essays in the book are deeply influenced by my growing fascination with the rhetorical aspect of contemporary American poetry. "The 'Prose Lyric'" carries some of the notions developed in "'The Found' in Contemporary Poetry" a step further and even hazards, in the light of contemporary poetic practice, a "definition" of poetry. It is a definition that I, too, find extreme; yet it is the definition of poetry that, I have to conclude, most poets implicitly adhere to what they write in verse because it is deduced from examples of how poets are actually using verse.

Although "Stephen Dunn and the Realist Lyric" does not tackle directly the issue of our poetry as rhetoric, I wrote the essay because, in the earlier essays, I found myself time and time again turning to poems by Dunn as examples of rhetorical resourcefulness. I came to believe that, of all our contemporaries, Dunn exhibits the greatest sensitivity to poetry as rhetoric and demonstrates the greatest rhetorical inventiveness, an inventiveness that allows him to write directly out of his own life instead of playing the kinds of beautiful but detached post-modernist games that a poet such as Ashbery plays.

"'Instant Wordsworth,'" the most recently completed piece in the book, is the only one that was designed specifically for this collection. Although the actual occasion for the essay is the opportunity to refute an attack that the critic Marjorie Perloff launched at a poem by Richard Hugo, I found that the implications of the attack were so broad that the essay seemed also to be a convenient forum in which to round out some of the themes raised in the other essays. Thus the last essay relates the rhetoric of the contemporary lyric to the question of what constitutes the post-modernist mode; it attempts rather casually to suggest a historical frame within which to fit that rhetoric; and it suggests also how neglect of the rhetorical aspect of poetry can lead to a distorted and oversimplified picture of what contemporary American poetry is all about.

The primary thrust of the book, however, is not to defend a rhetorical approach to our poetry as better or worse than any other approach. As I have already mentioned, the essays emerged independently and are simply attempts to put down and to examine in a reasonably orderly and thorough way some of the questions that continue to nag me whenever I sit down to read or to write. Although the essays sometimes assert answers to these questions, I regard the answers as being, like the endings to poems, interesting conclusions to various lines of argument rather than prescriptions addressed to the world at large. Like the endings of poems, whatever charm these conclusions possess will spring from the way in which they were derived rather than from their application outside the context in which they arose. For me, the process of writing the essays, of trying to think through various issues and to illustrate them, was absorbing; and the close engagement with some beautiful poems that the process demanded made it exciting. If the reader comes away from the book with nothing else, I would hope it is some sense of fresh or renewed appreciation for the poems that he or she encountered in the essays.

Note
1. My use of the masculine generic here, as throughout the book, is in no way intended to imply that college teaching and the writing of poetry are exclusively male activities in a male world. Wherever I have used it, the reader should know that I found it, although less cumbersome than "he or she" or "he/she," a regrettable embarrassment.

THE RHETORIC OF THE
CONTEMPORARY LYRIC

One

"AFFECTED NATURALNESS" AND THE POETRY OF SENSIBILITY

A sobering exercise today is to skim through the mid-century edition of Louis Untermeyer's *Modern American Poetry* (1950). Whereas it contains many of the great modernist poems by T. S. Eliot, Ezra Pound, William Carlos Williams, and company, it also contains a fair number of poems that, if submitted to any graduate poetry workshop today, would be scoffed at. With perfect aplomb the workshop would dismiss these poems on the grounds that they were "jingly" or "didactic" or "forced" or "sentimental." I am thinking, for example, of the work of Elizabeth Maddox Roberts, whose poem "The Sky" begins:

> I saw a shadow on the ground
> And heard a bluejay going by;
> A shadow went across the ground,
> And I looked up and saw the sky.

I am thinking of the work of Elinor Wylie, whose poem "The Eagle and the Mole" starts out:

"'Affected Naturalness' and the Poetry of Sensibility" originally appeared in *College English* 41 (December 1979): 398–408. Copyright © National Council of Teachers of English. Reproduced, with minor changes, by permission.

> Avoid the reeking herd,
> Shun the polluted flock,
> Live like that stoic bird,
> The eagle of the rock.

I am thinking of the work of William Rose Benét, whose poem "Night" begins:

> Let the night keep
> What the night takes,
> Sighs buried deep,
> Ancient heart-aches,
> Groans of the lover,
> Tears of the lost;
> Let day discover not
> All the night cost!

It would be with considerable reluctance that the workshop would concede that this kind of verse was even "poetry" at all; and I have to confess that all three of these excerpts leave me cold, too. But if I question my taste at all, I have to find my dislike of this poetry more than slightly unnerving; for not only were these poets contemporaries of Eliot and Pound, they were not half so unsophisticated as they sound to us now. They were in touch with the mainstreams of literary fashion. Indeed, as Untermeyer's headnotes demonstrate, they were, in their time, considered as "promising" as any of our "promising" contemporary younger poets, as promising, say, as any of the poets under age forty presented in Daniel Halpern's *American Poetry Anthology* (1975). It is unnerving because, if such promising writers could be so totally eclipsed—be relegated to laughing-stocks—in such a short time, it could happen to anybody or to any style.

It seems obvious, even self-evident, that particularly among poets fashion often limits the ability to appreciate worn-out styles of verse, especially if those styles are comparatively recent. But how severe is this limitation, and how is it rationalized? To try to answer these questions, let us imagine how the Roberts poem would be criticized in a graduate poetry workshop:

> I saw a shadow on the ground
> And heard a bluejay going by;
> A shadow went across the ground,
> And I looked up and saw the sky.

The main objection to the first stanza—to the entire poem, in fact—would be that the craft that went into it is too obtrusive. The poem cannot be spoken in a natural voice: it is too pretty, too contrived to be taken as a serious or urgent statement. It would be pointed out that the heavy redundancies in stanza one exist mainly to flesh out its prosodic pattern, that the more natural way of presenting the content of the stanza would read something like "The shadow of a bluejay sailed across the ground. I noticed the sky."

How might the rest of the poem be handled? The remaining three stanzas of the Roberts original are as follows:

> It hung up on the poplar tree,
> But while I looked it did not stay;
> It gave a tiny sort of jerk
> And moved a little bit away.

> And farther on and farther on
> It moved and never seemed to stop.
> I think it must be tied with chains
> And something pulls it from the top.

> It never has come down again,
> And every time I look to see,
> The sky is always slipping back
> And getting far away from me.

Below is the kind of "improved" version that might emerge from our workshop:

> Along the ground
> the bluejay's shadow
> sails. But I
> notice the sky
> hung in the poplar tree.
> It jerks, moving
> away. The sky
> is lifting away from me
> never to come down
> but to keep slipping
> back, always,
> the sky getting
> away like the wild
> bluejay.

The effects of all the changes are to make the conscious craft that went into the poem less obvious and to give the statement an air of greater urgency, greater immediacy, as if the narrator were re-experiencing the occasion of her poem even as she uttered it. The strict, too regular, wooden meter of the original has been eliminated in an effort to give the poem a more natural voice, one closer to unpremeditated speech. Unexpected line breaks have been introduced to modulate the pitch of the voice and the heft of the breath in order to give the delivery of the poem more tonality. Other evidences of the poet's straining for craft would be muted; for example, the ponderous chain metaphor would be absorbed into the verb "lifting." The entire narrative would be recast in the present tense to maximize its intensity.

Nevertheless, the final revision would be easily distinguishable from raw speech. Not only are its elements far more selective than those of conversation, but the workshop's version also still exhibits considerable unity of sound—particularly internal rhyme—and it exhibits distinct musical closure. It is obviously art, but art made to appear spontaneous, made to appear as if the speaker were excited, were moved enough that the poem's language and tempo had, by some organic process, assumed some of the shape of the speaker's excitement, had followed the curve of the speaker's process of recognizing her feelings.

Neither version of the Roberts poem is very good. But, as I hope the demonstration indicates, imagining how an outmoded poem might be edited by a poetry workshop in the 1970s can throw our present critical assumptions into relief. If these assumptions seem to be validated by the demonstration, it is because the Roberts poem, by any standard, is rather weak. The main canon of contemporary poetic style and its limitations are much more clearly seen if we try to apply the same exercise to a better poem. Imagine, then, how our graduate writing students would respond to Conrad Aiken's "Annihilation" as it was passed around on mimeographed sheets:

> While the blue noon above us arches
> And the poplar sheds disconsolate leaves,
> Tell me again why love bewitches
> And what love gives.
>
> Is it the trembling finger that traces
> The eyebrow's curve, the curve of the cheek?
> The mouth that quivers, while the hand caresses,
> But cannot speak?
>
> No, not these, not in these is hidden
> The secret, more than in other things:
> Not only the touch of a hand can gladden
> Till the blood sings.

It is the leaf that falls between us,
The bell that murmurs, the shadows that move,
The autumnal sunlight that fades upon us,
These things are love.

It is the "No, let us sit here longer,"
The "Wait till tomorrow," the "Once I knew"—
These trifles, said as you touch my finger
And the clock strikes two.

The world is intricate, and we are nothing.
It is the complex world of grass,
The twig on the path, a look of loathing,
Feelings that pass.

These are the secret; and I could hate you
When, as I lean for another kiss,
I see in your eyes that I do not meet you,
And that love is this.

Rock meeting rock can know love better
Than eyes that stare or lips that touch.
All that we know in love is bitter,
And it is not much.

Beginning with stanza one, it is immediately obvious that the workshop's objections to Aiken's highly developed style will be more subtly pervasive and far-reaching than were its objections to the crudity of the Roberts poem, that current taste in poetry—academic taste, at least—is founded on assumptions that go deeper than the question of obtrusive craft. "The blue noon above us arches" would probably be changed to "The blue noon arches above us." "Its" would replace "disconsolate" in line two. Lines three and four would be dropped.

These changes alone would invoke our most fundamental biases about poetic style. The changes in the first two lines are toward artlessness, away from Aiken's deliberately literary style with its occasionally stilted word order and its use of the threadbare Pathetic Fallacy. Indeed, if there be any one hallmark of poetic style in the 1970s, it is its *studied* artlessness. The roots of this fashion are complex, but it is largely the result of a continuing reaction against the kind of highly wrought, academic New-Critical verse so prevalent in the 1950s and early 1960s, the kind of verse epitomized in *New Poets of England and America* (1957). In much of that poetry, which was heavily influenced by Eliot's notion that great poetry requires suppression of the author's individual personality, the tone is that of a refined and cultivated irony, irony that constitutes such a dense mask that the reader feels confronted not with a human voice but with an elaborate contraption, one that with a boost from the New Critics would, as Eliot wished, assume a significance independent of the life or sensibility of its author. The early collections of Richard Wilbur epitomize this poetic at its best, as in, for example, his poem "Mind":

> Mind in its purest play is like some bat
> That beats about in caverns all alone,
> Contriving by a kind of senseless wit
> Not to conclude against a wall of stone.
>
> It has no need to falter or explore;
> Darkly it knows what obstacles are there,
> And so may weave and flitter, dip and soar
> In perfect courses through the blackest air.
>
> And has this simile a like perfection?
> The mind is like a bat. Precisely. Save
> That in the very happiest intellection
> A graceful error may correct the cave.

Like the one above, most of the New-Critical poems set up shop as essays, debating the merits of abstract ideas and exercising a metaphysical brand of wit. The poet's personality remains on the sidelines. Instead of saying "I feel" or "I think," the voice speaking the poem is apt to refer to such entities as "mind" or "the tall camels of the spirit." This poetic assumes that the concerns of a poem should transcend the petty, sweltering concerns of the individual. The forward movement within such poems is apt to be logical, dialectical rather than narrative. The form is static. The prosody is brilliant and meant to be noticed.

The problem of how much conspicuous artfulness a poem should display arrises in the 1960s with what A. Poulin, Jr., has termed "the personalization of poetry," a process that he describes as follows:

> The major difference between modernist and contemporary poetry is that the latter is more intimate and personal. The elements of the modernist poem worked toward assuring a distance between the poet and his subject, the poet and his poem. From persona to tradition, each was a formal, emotional and intellectual means for the poet's objectification of his subject, emotion and medium. The unique personality of the poet, his more intimate experiences and emotions were not only absent, indeed they were virtually taboo, and in the hands of lesser poets such an attitude resulted in a depersonalized and inhuman versification.[1]

But the more personal a poem is—the more a poem purports to be about the self of the author—the more the question of how sincere the poem sounds will be a factor in our judgment of it. And the greater the requirement for sincerity is, the more questionable will be the role of craft in a poem. With his customary acuity, Poulin summarizes this issue well:

> Moreover, in the work of some poets, technique and craftsmanship cause more doubt as to just how personal poetry can be; for by drawing formal attention, even the most personal poem reminds the reader that it is a fabrication. Like any art, personal poetry is a selective, calculated and public

gesture, a formal utterance for which the poet selects a voice, one which is as approximate to his own as is manageable.[2]

The issue of how to combine craft with sincerity is also everywhere implicit in Stanley Plumly's two-part essay, "Chapter and Verse." In this brilliant review of younger American poetry in the 1970s, Plumly characterizes the central options facing the American poet as problems of rhetoric. In his own words, Plumly attempts first "to sort out, through young and very recent examples, one reading of free verse—a verse preoccupied with its own voice and rhetoric, the voice of the emotion, a voice tested by its ability to create and control tone"; but, asserts Plumly, "the language of emotion . . . is expressly different from the language of the image." Thus, opposed to what Plumly labels "the prose lyric"—a poetry founded on the rhetoric of "voice"—is a poetic based on what he labels "the rhetoric of silence"—a poetic in which the image rather than the voice conveys the content of a poem. One of the main themes of Plumly's essay is an ongoing demonstration that the capabilities of the two rhetorics are mutually exclusive. As Plumly puts it, "the really essential difference between poets preoccupied with a free verse voice and a verse emblem is a difference of the degree to which the poet will admit himself into his poem—and the terms of such a testament. . . . The speaking voice, as a free verse instrument, is too flawed, it would seem, to handle both itself and symbol simultaneously."[3]

After reminding us that "the history of the Modernist movement in poetry is a history of the image," Plumly adduces poems by Daniel Halpern, Laura Jensen, Sandra McPherson, and other younger poets, poems that in Plumly's words attain to the condition of "absolute poetry, an autotelic poetry, like the Urn itself," which "is finally an abstract poetry—a poetry whose ultimate concern, through its images, objects, its absorbing emblem, is with that ulterior dimension we call *idea*."[4] One of his star witnesses for such a poetry is Sandra McPherson's "Wearing White":

> The old dogged ways of writing poems
> cover with snow. Juncos, bodied like lynx tails,
> fly out of the empty prison.
>
> Dipping his hand in blood the taxidermist complains
> nothing will stay on this white. He raises
> a frozen wasp by a leg, beginning to move.
>
> On maples the sensory tips say: we refuse,
> not another experiment. They wonder if they are not
> warped by feeling. Frosting the interior
>
> that faces them a pocket watch hangs, stopped
> and silver. It listens as the leaves clatter
> into glassy cornerings. An idea
>
> of what to do with an idea: I am wearing white—
> the height of the heart of a tree in my boreal
> clothes. My seamstress sets down
>
> her needle, with a headache. Like windows
> painted shut, snow everywhere hardens. My hands
> are cold, and they must keep cold, like milk.

True, this poem relies heavily on "emblem" and displays a number of modernist features. The voice of the author is peripheral, the tactics of the poem are symbolist, and the poem relies on a modernist fragmentary form, expecting the reader to supply the missing connections. But the differences between this poem and modernism are at least as conspicuous as their similarities. First of all, the poem has a personal feel to it. The present tense lends it a narrative ring.

We sense that we are suffering through an instant with the speaker and that the speaker is probably the author because she refers to the activity in which she is presently engaged: writing a poem. As "the seamstress sets down/ her needle, with a headache," the author is winding up her poem, which is about trying to write by force of will—the exhaustion that results from such a mechanical operation of the spirit. More important, however, is the poem's lack of conspicuous artifice. Its rhetorical strategy is to masquerade as a series of images whose coherence is not consciously contrived but is the result of the author's superior sensibility. The end product is, like much contemporary poetry—particularly the kind being fostered in university creative-writing programs—a "poetry of sensibility," a cultivated attempt to imitate spontaneous vision, to produce through carefully muted craft the illusion of urgency. This is why "Wearing White" looks so rough-hewn. Were McPherson really attaining, as Plumly suggests, to an "absolute poetry," a pure, timeless Byzantine artifact, it would embrace the high gloss—the chiming redundancies—of brilliant artifice. But the poem cannot because it is too personal. It is, to borrow the slightly depreciating term that Wendell Berry coins in his essay "The Specialization of Poetry," a "wordself."[5]

Although Plumly is right on target when he characterizes the main questions of poetic form right now as questions of rhetoric, it seems to me that he concentrates a little too hard on "the degree to which the poet will admit himself into his poem" instead of on the real question, "the terms of such a testament." As a result, in the second part of "Chapter and Verse," Plumly may represent the poetry under discussion as considerably less "personal" than it really is; for, as Poulin says, most contemporary poets admit themselves into their poems to a relatively high degree. What varies is how directly or how obliquely they make reference, within their text, to themselves. The less direct their reference, the more a poem will, as

Plumly points out, depend on image rather than on narrative "voice," and the greater the risk that the poem will seem contrived and therefore "insincere"; because for a writer to adopt an image or metaphor as correlative to his state of mind requires some aesthetic distance between himself and his material: it requires premeditation. The problem facing the poet is how to conceal that fact. Thus, if a poet's main subject is his self, whether he uses "the rhetoric of silence" or the rhetoric of "voice," in either case he must roughen the surface of his art in order to preserve that sense of personal urgency that any "personal" statement must retain if it is to be rhetorically effective, if it is to seem to have a valid *raison d'être* at all.

Although it is true that such poets as Theodore Roethke and W. D. Snodgrass have written convincingly in a personal mode while retaining many or all of the elements of traditional prosody, to do so not only is extremely difficult, but also it does not always work. Roethke's more plastic, free-form poems such as "The Lost Son" seem considerably more authentic than such highly wrought pieces as "In a Dark Time." As for "Heart's Needle," the portions that work are sheer miracle—poetry that will endure—but some of it sounds a bit sententious. As Mark Strand puts it:

> I can say that we distrust rhyme because it sounds a little tinny, a little false, a little decorative, and a little unnatural. The point of writing a version of plain-style verse, it seems, is to affect as much as possible the naturalness of conversation.[6]

In an article about the teaching of poetry writing, Albert Goldbarth more succinctly asks, "Does the poem, despite its technical ease, really sound earned and urgent . . . or does it have that ground-out-for-a-grade feel?"[7] It is significant, I think, that Goldbarth is concerned that a poem *sound* earned and urgent rather than whether or not it *be* earned and urgent. Similarly, Strand wants the poem only to *affect* naturalness.

A good example of such "affected naturalness" is Strand's own "Lines for Winter":

> Tell yourself
> as it gets cold and gray falls from the air
> that you will go on
> walking, hearing
> the same tune no matter where
> you find yourself—
> inside the dome of dark
> or under the cracking white
> of the moon's gaze in a valley of snow.
> Tonight as it gets cold
> tell yourself
> what you know which is nothing
> but the tune your bones play
> as you keep going. And you will be able
> for once to lie down under the small fire
> of winter stars.
> And if it happens that you cannot
> go on or turn back
> and you find yourself
> where you will be at the end,
> tell yourself
> in that final flowing of cold through your limbs
> that you love what you are.

At first the poem looks like an almost casual delivery. It has no scannable, prosodic pattern. It has no literary allusions. What end rhymes it has look accidental, though they sound pleasant. Except for "the tune your bones play" and "flowing of cold," the diction is not especially "literary." The tone is intimate, colloquial, established by the bleak "gets cold" instead of "grows cold." The poem looks as fluidly delivered, as "natural" as a pro golfer's 250-yard tee shot.

Indeed, one might say that the sensibility of the contemporary "pro" poet bears the same relation to the craft of composition that the body of a professional athlete bears to its conditioning and training. This poem wants to look like the feat of a "natural" athlete. On closer examination, however, it reveals itself as quite a crafty piece. The poem is an essay that in virtually every line poses the question of how (or whether) we should accept the fact that day by day we head a little closer to death. Its tactic is to pretend to answer the question, over and over. The voice speaking the poem could be speaking to itself in a monologue designed to be overheard, it could be addressing a single person, or it could be addressed directly to anybody listening. In fact, the voice is directed at all three audiences. It *is* the little chant that we "tell ourselves" from instant to instant because we have no choice. By revealing his own chant, the poet knows that he speaks for us, with us. It is as if everybody in the world were reciting this poem at once, whether they knew it or not, like people rubbing their hands together involuntarily to keep them warm.

Although the content of the poem is like that of an essay, it is presented dramatically rather than as exposition; it is presented as the quietly desperate, bemused, ironic interior monologue of a person in action, of a person doing anything. "And if it happens that you cannot/ go on or turn back/ and you find yourself/ where you will be at the end" is a deliberate ambush set for the reader. It takes effect as the reader, at first puzzled, realizes that only so long as one presumes to have any say in the matter—only so long as one presumes to be *able* to "tell yourself" to "go on"—does one entertain the illusion that one has the option of going on or turning back, of transcending time. But of course that option is not there. As the reader looks back through the poem, he notices that a suppressed clause that says something like "even though you can't" looms implicitly after each repetition of "tell yourself," that "where you will be at the end"—another ambush—is here, right now, anywhere, in the passing moment. The final force of the poem—a painful, yet also quietly hilarious, one—is to make us recognize that despite the futility of it we will go right on pretending to "tell ourselves," go right on reciting the same "poem" over and over again, just as the poem does—that in a sense it is our only poem.

Not only is Strand's poem rhetorically contrived, but it is so stuffed with music—with heavy internal rhyme and alliteration—that it is close to song. Even without the assistance of Strand's chant-like style of intonation, it musically coheres, it moans, and its sound clings to the ear. It constitutes, in fact, a highly artificial mode of speech. It fulfills the paradoxical requirements Strand imposes on verse: it preserves some semblance of "naturalness," yet it is highly "affected." In fact, the rather hypothetical way in which this poem dwells on the idea of death—hypothetical in that the poem is not occasioned by any particular death, but instead purports to be a testament of the poet's daily hypersensitivity to death—has a distinctly literary flavor. "Lines for Winter" is, despite its suave, off-the-cuff look, a highly literary poem on the most conventional literary theme there is: Death with a capital D.

We can now begin to anticipate the changes that our poetry workshop would require of Aiken, and also the rationale for those changes. "Annihilation" treats the conventional theme of Love in just as carefully cultivated a manner as Strand treats the conventional theme of Death, the only difference being that Aiken did not feel the need to "affect naturalness," to putty over the most obvious elements of craftiness as Strand has. Both poems are the work of a cultivated, overrefined sensibility, but Strand has attempted to disguise the degree of his refinement. Aiken, on the other hand, makes no bones about it: his poem is what our workshop would regard as blatantly—almost shamelessly—"literary." One senses that Strand might really prefer to write as Aiken does, but that current, academic poetic style forces him to mute his effects, to hide his art, to make it look as if he were not trying as hard as he is.

"The blue noon arches above us,/ the poplar sheds its leaves" evinces roughly the balance of artfulness and naturalness that currently defines our taste in poetic style. But why, as our workshop did, drop lines three and four? They announce the poem's theme too explicitly. The main culprit is the abstraction "love." Such abstractions are usually too explicit. This is why Strand's poem does not use the word "death," even though the theme of Death saturates it. The heresy of explicitness is a corollary to the general requirement of naturalness. Much of the "weakness" of the Aiken poem is that, in the midst of a dramatic situation—two lovers absorbed in each other under a shedding poplar—the speaker is carrying on an elegant and rather literary debate about the transience of Love. The mixture of essay and drama is entirely too artificial. If the speaker retains enough aesthetic distance from his own situation to debate it in courtly fashion, then the situation itself is not urgent enough to warrant speech. It is being trumped up, exploited for literary purposes, and the speaker is therefore not being entirely sincere. If the poet is to seem sincere, he must move as a natural athlete. He must seem to move instinctively, without knowing completely what he is doing; otherwise he will resemble a plotting rhetorician, not a person to trust. The theme of the poem must be so discreetly buried that the attentive reader will think that *he* has discovered it *for* the poet. The coherence of a poem around a theme must seem to be the inadvertent (but of course inevitable) result of the poet's extraordinary sensibility. The theme must be almost wholly implicit.

We can now rather easily edit the rest of Aiken's poem. From stanza two, we can salvage "your trembling finger traces my eyebrow's curve. Your lips quiver. We can't speak." "The curve of the cheek," which is redundant and weaker than "the eyebrow's curve," is, like "the hand that caresses," there only to flesh out a mechanical, prosodic pattern. Such redundancies also undermine the drama and immediacy of the narrative; they jeopardize the illusion of its urgency.

All of stanza three must go. It is too abstract, too explicit, too expository. "The blood sings" is too obviously literary and therefore too artificial to be tolerated. Indeed, by the contemporary canon, stanza three is not "poetry."

Our hypothetical workshop would also delete most of stanza four. The poet should not reintroduce the falling-leaf motif this self-consciously because that makes us too conscious that the entire occasion of the poem is being trumped up, that it exists only for literature, that it is not of sufficient urgency to be above the need for deliberate embellishment. The reference to "autumnal sunlight" also must go. We already know that it is autumn because leaves are being shed. To reiterate autumn is to dwell on it too heavily, too deliberately, to convert it into standard literary currency. If it is "noon," then the light cannot be "fading" unless it be figuratively, which is both a worn-out figure and too explicit. The "bell" would have to go. Bells "murmur" only in romantic literature. "These things are love" is too abstract, expository, explicit. "The shadows . . . move" is the one detail our workshop might salvage.

Except for "you touch my finger," stanza five would be deleted entirely. Its syntax would be deemed too artificial, too contrived, too elaborate to be the speech of a man reliving an emotional moment. If we take "the clock" in the last line as symbolizing Time, the last line of stanza five makes a neat pun of "strikes two"; but it is untrue to the poem's time sense that it be two o'clock now if, only a few lines above, it was "noon." Moreover, the very possibility of such an elegant pun must be forestalled because, by suggesting an obtrusion of too much conscious craft into the making of the poem, it would impugn the poem's purported pathos.

From stanza six our workshop might try to salvage the expression "the complex world of grass." The first line not only is too explicit, too abstract; it also is too didactic. The sensibility can feel, but it is not supposed to think, for we cannot plan our feelings; if it cannot think, neither can it preach. The didactic heresy is thus, like the heresy of explicitness, another form of insincere calculation, of premeditation. "The twig on the path" is redundant stuffing, weaker than "the complex world of grass." "A look of loathing" is too explicit. "Feelings that pass" is too abstract, too explicit.

Stanza seven our workshop would edit less strenuously. "These are the secret" would have to go, as would the last line of the stanza. The remaining material would probably be salvaged in roughly its present form.

Most of stanza eight would be deemed too explicit, too didactic. But the concrete image of "rock meeting rock" would be salvaged, and the class would attempt somehow to work the import of the last three lines back into the very imagery of the poem, to implicate it into the poem's dramatic situation.

And here, with the salvaged parts incorporated and reworked, is roughly the version our workshop would deliver:

> Your finger trembles
> as it traces
> the curve of my eyebrow.
> > We can't
> speak. Above, the blue noon
> arches. The poplar sheds
> its leaves. Shadows
> move through the complex world
> of the grasses. Your lips
> tremble. I touch
> your cheek. You
> touch my finger. And I could
> hate you,

when, as I lean
for another kiss, I see
in your eyes, that we
can't even touch as well
as the rocks.

Obviously this is worse than the original. But that is not the point of this exercise. In its own way, the style of this version is as mannered as Aiken's. It is as mannered as any prevalent style of the moment. And what Frank O'Hara once remarked about music may apply to poetry: "There is about as much freedom in the composition of music as there is in a prison recreation yard."[8]

Notes

1. A. Poulin, Jr., ed., *Contemporary American Poetry*, 2d ed. (Boston: Houghton Mifflin, 1975), p. 460.

2. Ibid., pp. 461–62.

3. Stanley Plumly, "Chapter and Verse: Part II," *American Poetry Review* 7 (May–June 1978): 24.

4. Ibid., p. 29.

5. Wendell Berry, "The Specialization of Poetry," *Hudson Review* 27 (Spring 1975): 14.

6. "Conversation with Mark Strand," *Ohio Review* 13 (Winter 1972): 58.

7. Albert Goldbarth, "Confusing But Never Confused," *Field* 18 (Spring 1978): 58.

8. Unpublished letter to Bill Berkson, 12 August 1962, quoted in Marjorie Perloff, "In Favor of One's Time (1954–61): Frank O'Hara," *American Poetry Review* 6 (May–June 1977): 10.

Two

THE "FOUND" IN CONTEMPORARY POETRY

One of the common misconceptions regarding "found" art if it be literary "art" is that it is merely a self-conscious, *avant garde* shock tactic. As Ronald Gross, a notable practitioner of found poetry, writes, "Found poetry turns the continuous verbal undertone of mass culture up full volume for a moment, offering a chance to see and hear with a shock of recognition."[1] A good example of what Gross means is his "Sonnet: Painful Hemorrhoids?"

> All too often, humans who sit and stand
> Pay the price of vertical posture. Sitting
> And standing combine with the force of gravity,
> Exerting extra pressure on veins and tissues
> In and around the rectal area.
> Painful, burning hemorrhoids result.
> The first thought of many sufferers
> Is to relieve their pain and their discomfort.
>
> Products, however, often used for this
> Contain no anesthetic drug at all, or one
> Too weak to give the needed pain relief,

"The 'Found' in Contemporary Poetry" originally appeared in *Georgia Review* 33 (Summer 1979): 329–41, and is reproduced here, with minor changes, by permission.

Or only lubricate. But now, at last
There is a formulation which provides
pain-killing power, prolonged relief, on contact.

John Robert Columbo defines found poetry a little differently:
"Found poem: A passage of prose presented as a poem. The trans-
formation usually involves rearranging the lines on the page."[2] Although Columbo does not say so, the notion of shock, of an egre-
gious displacement of some *objet trouvé* from its customary banal
context into the rarified context of high art, is implicit in the words
"prose presented as a poem": an onion presented as an apple. A good
example of a found poem, by Columbo's definition, is David Antin's
"Code of Flag Behavior":

the flag should never be displayed with the union down   except
          as a sign of distress
the flag should never touch anything underneath it
such as the ground   the floor   or water
it should never be carried laid out flat or horizontally
but always aloft and free
it should not be festooned   drawn back   or up in folds
but allowed to fall free
the flag should never be used to cover a ceiling
it should never have placed on it   or attached to any part of it
any mark insignia letter word figure design picture drawing
of any nature whatsoever
the flag should never be used as a receptacle for
receiving holding carrying or delivering
it should not be used for advertising purposes   and
when the flag is in such condition that it is no longer fit for use
as an emblem of display
it should be destroyed
in a dignified way
preferably by burning

This is fun; but there is, I believe, a broader and less trivial way of construing the found in poetry, which may indicate the degree to which the aesthetic of the found has spread and, rather insidiously, I think, come to influence the assumptions—perhaps "conventions" is the better word—that govern current poetic form and that poets now take so for granted that they are scarcely aware of applying them.

As an illustration of this broader sense of the found and of the rather fluid sense in which I am going to apply it, let us re-examine that famous poem by Robert Creeley, "I Know a Man":

> As I sd to my
> friend, because I am
> always talking,—John, I
>
> sd, which was not his
> name, the darkness sur-
> rounds us, what
>
> can we do against
> it, or else, shall we &
> why not, buy a goddamn big car,
>
> drive, he sd, for
> christ's sake, look
> out where yr going.

Since this poem was written, the range of workable verse conventions has been so extended and ratified through use that the assumptions behind the poem seem almost commonplace; but I would like to ask here the question I asked myself when I first encountered this piece years ago: How should one read it? It looks like a fragment of conversation or perhaps a pastiche of related fragments—a condensation of a much longer conversation. If it were not set as verse, it would hardly resemble poetry at all. It is not sonorous. It is not rhythmically lovely in any orthodox sense. It has no beautiful images. It does not have a graceful forward movement or a stately shape. Indeed, its claim to the title of "poetry" lies in none of the intrinsic characteristics of language we traditionally associate with that title. In fact, it does not even appear to be intelligible. What is it about?

At this point, our critical instincts assert themselves. Perhaps through a "close reading" of this poem we can at least discover some connection between its elements. And so, guided by this hunch and by the faith that a poem's "form" and "content" are supposed to be more or less interchangeable, we dutifully grind out the following explication: The narrator is nervous and absentminded, so preoccupied with his own lugubrious existential despair—with The Big Questions, with the certitude of "darkness," with the surrounding philistinism epitomized by the American "big car"—that he cannot even keep his mind on the road. He narrowly avoids an accident. The poem is thus a cautionary parable whose point is, Don't get so carried away by self-indulgent, grandiose philosophical pessimism that you forget to "look/ out where yr going," that you forget to pay attention to banal immediacies. The poem's form reinforces its content. The run-together syntax of the first stanza, its mumbling quality, and its aimless line breaks all reflect the speaker's habit of drifting off. The line breaks of the second stanza make the voice come down hard and melodramatically on "surROUNDS" and "WHAT can we DO aGAINST it." The third stanza drifts off into mumbling distraction. The jarring yell of the fourth stanza is created almost wholly by deliberate placement of words around line breaks.

This way of making sense of the poem sounds vaguely plausible; but I must confess that the reading above—the only reading I can wring from the poem—seems to me to be adventitious. In fact, I am certain that, by applying standard New-Critical techniques, one could invent a plausible justification for any collection of words assembled as verse, isolated on the page, and asserted as a "poem." Confronted with gibberish, one could import heavy concepts such as "entropy" in order to argue that the poem was about its own incoherence, that its content was, like the content of all true poetry, inseparable from its form.

What is it, then, when we are confronted with the Creeley poem or with any poem, that makes us struggle to uncover, no matter how hidden it may be, that thread of connectedness that will reveal the poem to be all of a piece? The obvious answer is "convention." Literary convention, by definition, is changeable, as changeable as taste itself (indeed, "convention" may be merely a corollary of "taste"), and, at the present time, in the late 1970s, the ruling convention of our verse—more fundamental than rhyme and rhythm—is our assumption that verse asserts closure, that there must be some reason for isolating only *these* words together in the middle of a page. To put it differently, the way in which a piece of literature is framed—as prose, as verse, as found art, or as a prose poem—has a decisive influence on our expectations and determines which strategy we will use in reading it, *regardless of the inherent properties of its language.* As a demonstration of this, imagine starting to read what you believed to be a short story entitled "I Know a Man," which begins:

As I sd to my friend, because I am always talking,—John, I sd, which was not his name, the darkness surrounds us, what can we do against it, or else, shall we & why not, buy a goddamn big car.

Drive, he sd, for christ's sake, look out where yr going, there's a cop on yr tail.

What about the stash? I sd.

Too late, he sd, better pull over, man.

Shit, I sd.

Shhh, he sd, for christ's sake, don't let the fuzz hear that, here he comes.

& this fuzz comes up with this spiral notebook & leather creaking like a
mountie.
Ok fella, outa the car, he sd.
So I got out in the milky marin light & John got out while fuzzy sorta
smiled & . . . .

Although the delicate network of alleged consistencies so essential
to justifying the poem "I Know a Man" is still intact, it is irrelevant
in this context. Unless it be framed as verse, asserted to be a "poem,"
"I Know a Man" can be something else. Its effectiveness as art is
almost entirely dependent on how it is framed, not on properties
inherent in its language. On the other hand, one could write out
most of Theodore Roethke's poems as prose, and not only would the
poems retain most of their beauty, but also most people would recognize them as poems written out in prose because certain obvious
characteristics of sound and diction that have been conventionally
associated with verse would survive, albeit less comfortably, within
the new frame. Consider, for example, a prose frame for Roethke's
"The Waking":

I wake to sleep, and take my waking slow. I feel in my fate what I cannot
fear. I learn by going where I have to go.
We think by feeling. What is there to know? I hear my being dance from
ear to ear. I wake to sleep, and take my waking slow.
Of those so close beside me, which are you? God bless the Ground! I shall
walk softly there, and learn by going where I have to go.
Light takes the Tree; but who can tell us how? The lowly worm climbs
up a winding stair; I wake to sleep and take my waking slow.
Great Nature has another thing to do to you and me; so take the lively
air, and, lovely, learn by going where to go.
This shaking keeps me steady. I should know. What falls away is always.
And is near. I wake to sleep, and take my waking slow. I learn by going
where I have to go.

It is in reliance on the verse frame to compel meaning that the
Creeley poem most resembles found poetry or, indeed, all kinds of

found art. An ordinary smooth stone, surrounded by a five-hundred-dollar frame, hung in a prestigious museum and entitled "Seabirth" or "Psyche" (or anything fancy) strikes us far differently than if we had picked it up off a beach. A Campbell Soup can, isolated in the Museum of Modern Art and asserted as art, seems to acquire more aesthetic significance than it has in its rightful place on a grocery shelf. The Creeley poem is not, of course, "found" in the pure sense that Gross's advertisement poems are "found" or that a framed stone or a soup can is. Unlike the Gross poem, it was originally intended as a poem. Unlike a soup can, it is intended as art. Unlike a stone, it is man-made. In fact, some artful characteristics—the selectivity of its imagined conversation and the tactical way its lines break—are inherent in the work rather than in the frame; but the importance of framing in the poem's overall effectiveness is relatively high, so high that, *without the sense of closure enforced by the assumed nature of verse, "I Know a Man" could not come off.*

The Creeley poem is comparatively recent; but the development of the convention whereby the closure of the verse frame itself creates "meaning," automatically converting every element within the frame into part of a single, overall metaphor, begins with the modernists, most obviously with Eliot and Williams. Indeed, this may be their most far-reaching legacy in the development of poetic form. If there be any one single work that legitimized the poetic technique of leaving out connectives and letting coherence be asserted implicitly within the verse frame, it would have to be *The Waste Land.* Although most of the beauty and power of that poem still resides within its materials, within the frame, parts of that poem, conspicuously in the second section, are not inherently poetical and derive their relevance almost exclusively from context, for example, the passage beginning with line 139:

> When Lil's husband got demobbed, I said—
> I didn't mince my words, I said to her myself,

HURRY UP PLEASE ITS TIME
Now Albert's coming back, make yourself a bit smart,
He'll want to know what you done with that money he gave you
To get yourself some teeth. He did, I was there.
You get them all out, Lil, and get a nice set,
He said, I swear, I can't bear to look at you.

A number of William Carlos Williams' most famous poems are heavily dependent on framing the found. "The Red Wheelbarrow" is such a poem. Written as prose, it is trivial:

> so much depends upon a red wheelbarrow glazed with rainwater beside the white chickens.

Another is the famous "Poem":

> As the cat
> climbed over
> the top of
>
> the jamcloset
> first the right
> forefoot
>
> carefully
> then the hind
> stepped down
>
> into the pit of
> the empty
> flowerpot.

In prose, this is still fine writing, but some of its peculiar magic is gone; the image somehow lacks the preternatural clarity, the rapt concentration on process that is achieved through the isolation of narrow lines on the blank page:

As the cat climbed over the top of the jamcloset first the right forefoot carefully then the hind stepped down into the pit of the empty flowerpot.

Perhaps the best example of Williams' successful exploitation of a verse format as a frame for the found is "This Is Just to Say":

THIS IS JUST TO SAY

I have eaten
the plums
that were in
the icebox

and which
you were probably
saving
for breakfast.

Forgive me
they were delicious
so sweet
and so cold

It is easy enough to believe that this poem is found in the most literal sense, that it is merely a transcription of an actual note stuck to an icebox. What is gained by putting it into verse and according it the preciosity, the special status of isolation, is not in this case a set of connections leading toward an elegant explication: it is a coyness of tone caused by the displacement of a rhetorical strategy from a banal context into a rarified one. As a poem, the icebox note becomes an evocative tidbit of self-revelation, seasoned by the hint that such human foibles as the desire to sneak cold plums is grandly universal, is almost a sentimental truth. This evocativeness develops almost entirely from displacement of context rather than from any element *in* the poem. Indeed, it must be true almost by definition that the less imagery, the less figurative language, and the less rhythm in a poem, the more influence its frame, its closure, its sense of an "ending" is going to have on how we read it; and the more the poem is going to have to substitute in place of the orthodox rhetorical strategy of poetic conventions a found rhetorical strategy.

The most obvious examples of poems based on found rhetorical structures are poems whose forms mimic some other nonpoetic rhetorical form: a scrap of conversation, a letter, an icebox note, a recipe, a headline, an advertisement. Phil Dacey's "Form Rejection Letter," for example, is based on the format of a rejection slip:

> We are sorry we cannot use the enclosed.
> We are returning it to you.
> We do not mean to imply anything by this.
> We would prefer not to be pinned down about this matter.
> But we are not keeping—cannot, will not keep—what you
> sent us.
> We did receive it, though, and our returning it to you
> is a sign of that.
> It was not that we minded your sending it to us unasked.
> ....

A more widespread kind of found rhetorical strategy is the sort of poem that has come to be called "the poem of instruction," a format that, I believe, was virtually invented by Gary Snyder in his "Things to Do" poems. The format mimics any list of directions, and the reason for its popularity among contemporary poets probably is that the instructional format, unlike most other formats, does not narrowly restrict style and is therefore more acceptable than, say, an advertising format, which, if used as the basis for a poem's form, will invariably produce a travesty, something satirical. The instructional format, like Williams' icebox-note format, automatically converts every line into a metaphor, as in the following passage from the beginning of "Things to Do Around a Lookout":

> Wrap up in a blanket in cold weather and just read.
> Practise writing Chinese characters with a brush
> Paint pictures of the mountains
> Put out salt for deer
> Bake coffee cake and biscuit in the iron oven,
> Hours off hunting twisty firewood, packing it all back up and
>   chopping.
> Rice out for the ptarmigan and the conies
> Mark well sunrise and sunset—drink lapsang soochong.
> Rolling smokes. . . .

Just as the dislocation of format in Williams' "This Is Just to Say" lends every line an element of coy but charming self-consciousness so that the poem seems to be commenting not only on its author's mometary weakness for plums but also on the excusable, indeed almost praiseworthy, impulsiveness of all human nature, so does every line of the Snyder poem assume, in context, an apparent weight out of all proportion to its literal content: each line is a metaphor urging our active involvement and immersion in the world at large. Most of the power in Synder's catalogue is dependent solely on the fact that the list is in verse.

As a hypothetical example of how the most apparently random items can assume aesthetic meaning through framing, consider the following short catalogue, "Why Horace Likes to Live Alone": (1) When the Colts meet the Bears this Sunday, Horace can watch the entire game at home. (2) He can watch the game all afternoon and drink as much Blatz as he wants. (3) From now on Horace can hog the evening paper over supper. (4) And after supper he won't even have to dry a dish. (5) The dishes are fun. Not an intrinsically fascinating list. But retitled it can be rather more interesting—for example, as follows:

PORTRAIT OF AN ADULTERESS

When the Colts meet the Bears this Sunday
Horace can watch the entire game
at home. He can watch the game
all afternoon
and drink as much Blatz as he wants.
From now on, Horace can hog
the evening paper over supper.
And after supper
he won't even have to dry a dish.
The dishes are fun.

Every line, even the innocuous phrase "Colts meet the Bears," assumes added juicy significance if we imagine the words of the poem occurring in the mind of Horace's adulterous wife. Out of the most unpromising language, one can build something like a poem by hanging everything from a title. This is an easier and far more flexible method of "finding" poetry than mimicking other rhetorical forms is, and it is becoming an increasingly common technique for generating a poem. A good example of the technique at its crudest is Michael Dennis Browne's "Paranoia," which begins:

When you drive on the freeway, cars follow you.

Someone opens your mail, two hands
that come out of your shirt-sleeves.

Your dog looks at you, he does not like you.

At the driving test the cop is tired. He has sat up
all night, screening your dreams.

If you go to the zoo, be sure to take your passport.

A more subtle use of the technique may be seen in Stephen Dunn's "On Hearing the Airlines Will Use a Psychological Profile to Catch Potential Skyjackers":

> They will catch me
> as sure as the check-out girls
> in every Woolworth's have caught me, the badge
> of my imagined theft shining in their eyes.
>
> I will be approaching the ticket counter
> and knowing myself, myselves,
> will effect [*sic*] the nonchalance of a baron.
> That is what they'll be looking for.
>
> I'll say "Certainly is nice that the
> airlines are taking these precautions,"
> and the man behind the counter
> will press a secret button,
>
> there'll be a hand on my shoulder
> (this will have happened before in a dream),
> and in a back room they'll ask me
> "Why were you going to do it?"
>
> I'll say "You wouldn't believe
> I just wanted to get to Cleveland?"
> "No," they'll say.
> So I'll tell them everything,
>
> the plot to get the Pulitzer Prize
> in exchange for the airplane,
> the bomb in my pencil,
> heroin in the heel of my boot.

Inevitably, it'll be downtown for booking,
newsmen pumping me for deprivation
during childhood,
the essential cause.

"There is no one cause for any human act,"
I'll tell them, thinking *finally*,
a chance to let the public in
on the themes of great literature.

And on and on, celebrating myself, offering
no resistance, assuming what they assume,
knowing, in a sense, there is no such thing
as the wrong man.

To appreciate how heavily this poem depends on its title, imagine it
with a different title, say, "Entering the Airport" or "Baggage
Search." With either of these titles, the reader would be able to
follow the poem, but he would be apt to take the entire poem too
literally, to imagine the speaker feeling uncomfortable while approaching the airport security area. In fact, the words "On Hearing"
are the most important words in the title because once we realize
that the narrator is only imagining a scene that will never happen to
him, every detail of the fantasy is converted into metaphor, and we
realize that the poem is not about the literal threat authority poses
to one's person but rather about the poet's sense of the tenderness,
the vulnerability, of his inner life, no matter how innocuous, about
his realization of the preposterous, indeed comic, discrepancy between his inner life and his public persona. Like all the other examples I have given, Dunn's strategy is to use the verse frame to
enhance the metaphorical potential of relatively ordinary conversa-
tional language, even when there is almost nothing in the language
that seems especially suited to verse. In "On Hearing . . . " the use

of verse is otherwise present only to meet rather secondary requirements: to augment the self-parodying melodrama of the beginning and to highlight the deliberately weary, almost obligatory Whitmanesque gesture at the end, where Dunn imagines letting the amorphous substance of his inner life spill out into the stupid, literal glare of public analysis.

Dunn's poem is a relatively extreme example of the predominance of the strategy of the found in contemporary American poetry; but I think it is fair to say that never in the history of English-language verse has traditional prosody received less emphasis than it is receiving now, and never has metaphor received more. There are exceptions, but by and large the emphasis on metaphor—often deliberately spectacular metaphor—in American poetry of the 1970s is a natural outgrowth of the recession of music in favor of closure as the dominant convention that seems at times virtually to define "poetry." Whereas it used to be assumed that the fundamental *raison d'être* of verse is its ability, through measure and tempo, to approximate the intimate relationship between form and content found in song, the popular assumption now is that the capability of verse to assert closure, to compel a sense of an ending, and to imply figurative meaning is at least as fundamental. Contemporary poetry still strives to marry form and content; but the "feeling" in a poem, which has traditionally been borne by the "music" of verse as song, is now, more often than not, borne by metaphor.

So far, all the examples of poems that I have given here have been in verse; but the very term "prose poem" and the popularity of that format are further evidence of how prevalent among today's poets is the notion of a poem as merely a rhetorical strategy to find meaning, to create metaphor through closure, rather than as verse to create music. Indeed, if we take "poem" to mean "verse," then "prose poem" means "prose that asserts the closure (and metaphoric possibility) of verse." What is "prose," then? It could be defined negatively as "language that cannot be exhibited to advantage in a verse frame"; or, as I would prefer, it could be defined positively as "language that can be shown to greater advantage in a prose frame than in a verse frame." Consider, for example, Russell Edson's short prose poem, "A Performance at Hog Theatre":

> There was once a hog theatre where hogs performed as men, had men been hogs.
>
> One hog said, I will be a hog in a field which has found a mouse which is being eaten by the same hog which is in the field and which has found the mouse, which I am performing as my contribution to the performer's art.
>
> Oh let's just be hogs, cried an old hog.
>
> And so the hogs streamed out of the theatre crying, only hogs, only hogs . . .

Like most poems that depend heavily on framing, "A Performance" uses a "found" rhetorical strategy. With "There was once," it pretends to be a folktale. In its dialogue it mimics the novel or the short story. The displacement of these storytelling conventions, augmented by the prose-poem format, immediately converts Edson's statement into metaophor; thus, as does virtually every prose poem that I have encountered, it reads like a parable. The convention of "poem" as closure has been carried to its logical extreme: the poem that is all metaphor and that is without music.

Notes

1. *Open Poetry*, ed. Ronald Gross and George Quasha, (New York: Simon and Schuster, 1973), p. 431.
2. John Robert Columbo, "A Found Introduction," in ibid., p. 434.

Three

THE ABUSE OF THE
SECOND-PERSON PRONOUN

One of the most salient conventions to gather momentum in American poetry today is the deployment, in poem after poem, of an ambiguous "you" that could refer to the reader, that could convey the third-person-singular sense of "one," or that could be the poet—the narrator—referring to himself as "you" in a poem that, as Northrop Frye says of the typical "lyric" poem, features a narrator talking or musing to himself while all the time aware that his interior monologue is being overheard.

Such ambiguity is not, I think, accidental. In fact, it is probably this very ambiguity of reference that tempts a poet to substitute "you" for a pronoun with a more restricted range of reference; for the apparent bonuses are enormous. First of all, the second-person sense of "you" explicitly emphasizes whatever sense of audience the poem manages to generate. As a result, one would suppose that the reader, feeling that the poem were addressed to him personally, would enjoy a greater sense of intimacy with the speaker and a stronger sense of the narrator's speaking presence than if the syntax of the poem were governed by some other pronoun. James Wright, in the first sentence of his prose poem "Young Don't Want To Be Born," tries to assert such a relation with the declaration "I know

just how you feel." And, indeed, one suspects that the very confidence with which Wright proclaims kinship with us enables him to
deliver the rest of his poem, that perhaps the mere act of asserting
"you" in its second-person sense helps to spur a poet through the
lonely process of composition by providing him, in his solitude,
with the illusion of a listener, with the sense that he is speaking *to*
somebody, however ill-defined that somebody may be.

A second apparent advantage in deploying the ambiguous, or
blurred, "you" is that the third-person sense of "you" as "one," like
the expression "you know?" so often tagged onto the end of a sentence, emphasizes the purported universality of the proposition
where it occurs, and it does so in an unpremeditated, colloquial,
intimate tone that is far less pretentious than the sermonic "we."
"We" is more formal, more oratorical than contemporary poetic
rhetoric will comfortably allow. A poem that begins with "we" is
apt to sound too much like a Sunday-school essay: "We of the human
race. . . ." "We" may be appropriate in an essay, in a contrived argument, but, in its sense of "I-plus-the-plural-you," it does not go
naturally with the surge of emotional urgency a poem must imitate
if it is to seem sincere. For this reason also, the third-person "you"
is preferable to the indefinite pronoun "one," which in a poem would
sound unbearably stuffy and tweedy.

Ambiguity, then, is what tempts the poet to deploy the blurred-
you: He can seem to be addressing the reader as a special "you"; and
yet, retaining an intimate and urgent tone, he can seem also to
speak for the entire human race. He can simultaneously emphasize
particularity and universality at every juncture. He can have the
best of both worlds. He can be both personal and prophetic. And
this suggests a third apparent advantage to the blurred-you. By
using "you" for "I," the poet calls less attention to himself in his
poem. As a result, even if the poem contains sensitive, personal

material, the "you" may lessen the danger that the poet will sound self-pitying, overintrospective, whining, or that the entire poem will seem somehow "too personal" to be relevant to the general reader; for the blurred-you, by deflecting attention from the speaker, insures that the poet will not make a fool of himself.

This impulse—an impulse that is fairly widespread among poets now—to place the poet in a more peripheral position in the poem, is, I think, the result of a continuing reaction against the excesses of the confessional mode. It reflects how aware poets are now of the terrible limits to that mode. If confessional poems represented the ultimate reaction against the wry, reasoned verses of the 1950s epitomized in *New Poets of England and America* (1957), poetry of the 1970s has, in turn, begun to swing toward the pre-confessional classicism and is trying to find a less central position for the poet within his poem. The popularity of the blurred-you is indicative of a compromise that many poets are seeking to strike between a personal rhetoric and a less autobiographical kind of rhetoric appropriate to a cooler, more finely crafted poetry. Although, as we shall see, the blurred-you can validly be deployed, too often it is being misapplied by poets in poems that have a basically testimonial or a narrative character—poems that should remain in the first- or second-person singular. In such cases as these, the arguments against the blurred-you are remarkably similar to the standard arguments against regular use of the passive voice in expository prose.

As an example of how the blurred-you detracts from a poem, consider the following short piece by Philip Booth:

STILL LIFE

The new-cut key on the blue-paint table.
Your place now. The third floor door,
the stairwell turn no bed
could get up through. But did.

> After you get the boy to sleep
> you sit at the blue-paint table.
> Tea with nothing. No milk, no honey.
>
> Against the table: the small brass shine.
>
> By the time you lie back down
> on the same old mattress
> you've decided: strip the blue paint off,
> bring the whole thing back to natural.
> That's what you promise yourself you'll do.
> Do for yourself. For Christmas.

Booth is one of our very finest poets, and this poem is, I hasten to say, not typical of his work. Perhaps that is why I find it so disappointing. What could be a fine poem—a complex miniature portrait in which seemingly an entire period of a person's life is, through some luminous and mysterious economy, refined into a few somber images—is almost totally subverted because its rhetorical frame—a forthright set of cues for the reader as to who is speaking to whom, through what mask, and for what ostensible purpose—is blurred. The reader cannot decide how to take this poem unless he knows to whom "you" refers. There are three obvious possibilities: (1) "you" is a substitute for the first-person-singular pronoun, who is the poet himself, and the poem is therefore autobiographical; (2) "you" is a substitute for the first-person-singular pronoun, who is not the poet, but who is, like the speaker of William Carlos Williams' "The Widow's Lament in Springtime," a character distinct from the author; (3) "you" is intended in the second-person singular, it refers to a person whom the poet knows, and the poem is therefore a rather private, cryptic message addressed to that person. The third possibility seems the most likely—the poem has that feel to it—but then Booth should have titled it something like "To Jenny" or "To Harry."

Without such a cue, we have to assume that "you" is a substitute for the first-person pronoun, in which case, whether or not the speaker is the poet, the substitution kills most of the poem's feeling. "My place now" is far less wooden than "your place now." Similarly, "I lie . . . on the same old mattress" contains a note of wry resignation—the implicit question, Why am *I* doing this?—that is lost with "you lie." Every element of the poem gains emotional complexity and drama from the substitution of "I" for "you" because the speaking voice takes clear responsibility for what it is saying. The reader no longer has the sense that the poet is adventitiously hanging images and diction on some convenient but nondescript store-dummylike armature. The poem becomes a single human voice, and whether the speaker be fictional or real is of no consequence. A statement like "Tea with nothing. No milk. No honey" is far more arresting in the first-person singular than in some other person because it is so odd that the speaker should have chosen these details to mention about himself. To change "I" to "you" is to mute the force of the utterance in much the same way that a passionate and idiosyncratic speech is muted when recast as indirect discourse. It is a little bit like having Hamlet begin, "You think 'to be or not to be' is the question."

Why, then, if the speaker of "Still Life" is talking to himself, would Booth translate the poem into the blurred second person? Perhaps the poem is overcommitted to the repetition of certain vowel sounds: "you," "new," "blue," "through," "do." If so, then Booth has mistaken his priorities, neglecting the poem's overall rhetorical disposition (a primary consideration, a precondition for the poem's effectiveness) in favor of a few local effects (a secondary consideration, a matter of detail) such as the gentle play on "do it yourself" in the last line. In an overtly symbolist poem—a poem whose very subject matter is language—Booth's priorities might be proper, but this poem is in a realist tradition. My own suspicion is that the author wished to insist, by means of "you," against any possibility that the poem seem autobiographical; for there is no reason to suppose that the speaker is anybody but the poet himself. If the speaker were somebody other than the author, then Booth would have provided in his title some cue as to the age, identity, and gender of the speaker. Since all this information is excluded, we have to assume that the poet intended us to make the conventional deduction: that, when there is no explicit information to the contrary, a poem in the first person is mostly autobiographical. To be sure, "Still Life" is a beautiful, resonant title for the poem, but to sacrifice the exposition of essential context for resonance in a title is so seriously to confuse priorities that we would have to question the exercise of common sense at every other point in the poem, too. "Your place now," along with "The new-cut key," suggests that either the "you" has recently moved into the "place" or that, whether by divorce or death, the "you" is now suddenly the sole owner of the "place." Clearly, the phrase "Your place now" is swollen with emotional allusions, but the emotion is inaccessible to the reader so long as the poem's dramatic context is kept so ambiguous. "After you get the boy to sleep" is another such passage. If we had some idea of the age and gender of the speaker, we could interpolate and measure the emotion of the line. Should it have the gruff, understated tenderness of a father, or the tired tone of a young mother impatient for the "boy" to get to sleep so that she can pick up her own life? The only reason I can think of why an author would leave us guessing would be out of his mistaken impulse toward decorum because the poem's true context embarrassed him. The deployment of the blurred-you, then, would be an attempt by the poet not to take full responsibility for what he was saying. It would translate the poem into a kind of code, leaving it resonant with meanings and feelings for those initiated into its dramatic context, but inaccessible to the general reader. Perhaps Booth was worried lest the scale of the setting and the occasion be too modest to warrant their full exposure in the public domain, that the intimacy of the inner moment that the poem captures might be too quiet, too fragile, too "personal" to interest a stranger. Perhaps this is why the poem comes out in something close to the passive voice, sounding as if anybody had spoken it; for the fact is that in this poem, as in all the poems where it is abused—deployed to obscure responsibility—the blurred-you is a defensive tactic, and, like most defensive tactics, it betrays the author's anxiety by trying too hard. In its blurred sense, "you" grasps at the reader's collar, insisting too shrilly on his complicity, on his presence as a listening audience. In the sense of "one," it obscures the singularity of the poem's experience and protests far too loudly that the poem's subject has universality. Like all bravado, the blurred-you is a form of faking: it deliberately misrepresents the tenuous relation between reader and poet by exaggerating the purported intimacy of that relation and by exaggerating the poem's purported relevance to a general audience. At the same time, it lends the poem a cool, poised attitude, a veneer of public decorum that seems inappropriate to the poem's content. As a result, it calls into question the very assumption on which the poem's effectiveness hinges if it is going to pretend to some degree of personal testimony: the assumption of its absolute sincerity. To see how true this is, substitute the first-person-singular pronoun for "you" wherever it occurs and imagine the title as something like "Jenny's Song"; or imagine the poem as is, but addressed "To Jenny." Why is the first-person version so much better than the blurred-you version? Because the "I" is not defensive. Instead, it leaves strongly implicit (and therefore believable) the very speaker-to-reader bond about which Booth is so doubtful. Instead of overtly soliciting the reader's participation, instead of alluding to it, the first-person point of view simply assumes it. Thus, paradoxically, it generates a much more palpable sense of an audience than "you" simply by seeming to take the presence of an audience for granted. Similarly, by admitting how personal the poem is, the first-person pronoun ensures that, however limited may be the pertinence of the speaker's testimony to the life of the reader, it will sound authentic. The more in earnest the speaker seems—the more "relevant" a poem seems to be to the life of the speaker—the more "relevant" the reader will feel that it is to his own life. In other words, the more seriously a person seems to take himself, the more seriously he will be taken by other people. True earnestness is the mark of the best poetry. It is a commonplace that great poetry is easy to parody, but even that cliché underestimates the risk that the best poems take. Great poetry is usually so earnest that the poet is constantly on the verge of making a fool of himself. This is most obvious in the work of poets such as Theodore Roethke, Gerard Manley Hopkins, Dylan Thomas, or Walt Whitman, but it is true of all types of poetry: a poem such as Richard Wilbur's "Love Calls Us to the Things of This World" is as close to sounding ridiculous as, say, Sylvia Plath's "Daddy." It is this earnestness that a poet is apt to mute by substituting, for a first- or third-person pronoun, the suave "you"—the "you" that commits itself to nothing and can turn the finest poem into an empty, elegant-sounding workshop exercise.

Another example of a brilliant poem ruined merely by a pronoun is the following piece by Dennis Schmitz:

RABBITS

the urge to stroke the dead
    one back, handfeed life
to the animal
body even as its soft
    vision dilates,
your calluses pulling
fur like lint from the unmendable

flesh.   shake your head
      & coming back, hose the hutch
before your wife
six months pregnant sees

the rabbit.   later
      she can launder your sweaty
overalls & empty the few
      black rabbit
pellets your pockets
caught.   in the closet you
change & relishing the bachelor
scents of your underwear
      drop it to your father-in-law's
bathroom floor.   now your voice

weighs nothing though
      you sing.

This poem, like the other works in the collection in which it appears, is accompanied by the poet's account of how it was composed. Schmitz says that his poems "begin in free-association, but the sounds of the words are more important . . . than the pictures they make. I discover the subject as the poem develops."[1] When, a little later, Schmitz refers to the characters in the piece, he does so as distantly as if they were merely convenient armatures to be covered with language:

> Once I was able to start working at the poem again I could see some direction. The wife's assumed response, her misunderstanding in the gestures of emptying the pockets and redoing the disembodied overalls were clearer. The weakness of the wife is acnowledged to be the weakness of the husband. I still didn't know what the husband would do. But I was squeezing out words by the time I got to the end of the third stanza. It was natural that I would lose interest in the ideas. . . . I was able to finish the poem

because the last stanza came to me as I read over the third stanza. It sounded right after I tried a few different line breaks. That the father-in-law's bathroom be the place of revelation seemed appropriate, if a little too ironic. I thought that the conclusion had to be definite as an answer to the sequence of events in the poem.[2]

Although I think that "Rabbits" cries out to be in the first person, when one considers the seemingly Olympian detachment with which Schmitz refers to "the husband" and "the wife," as if they were characters he had invented, I am astonished that the poem is not in the third person. The most plausible reasons why it is not are that (1) the poem is, in fact, autobiographical, so much so that, even in his account of its composition, Schmitz cannot bring himself to disclose the true identities of the characters and that (2) the characters are, as Schmitz would have us believe, wholly invented; but, afraid that the poem would sound too clinical, too much like a story, in the third person, Schmitz has deliberately equivocated, replacing "he" with "you" in order to force the poem's rhetoric back toward the lyric mode, in order mechanically to add "feeling" to the narrative voice by leaving just the faintest suggestion that the voice could be that of a man musing to himself. To me, the poem's "feel" is mostly autobiographical. The material presented in the first stanza sounds heartrendingly authentic. Even if the reference to the father-in-law is invented, enough of the poem seems taken from first-hand experience that the piece still wants to be in the first person. In either case, however, the deployment of the blurred-you is a defensive tactic, a form of equivocation that subverts the poem. Like the passive voice, it is here used to obscure the author's responsibility for what he is expressing.

Occasionally, if an author is daring enough and skillful enough, he can almost get away with substituting the blurred-you for the first-person pronoun. Such a near miss is Michael Ryan's "This Is a Poem for the Dead."

THIS IS A POEM FOR THE DEAD

fathers: naked, you stand for their big faces,
mouths stuffed flat, eyes weighted, your miserable dick
sticking out like a nose. Dressed, you're more
of a mother making dinner: those old dirt bags,
the lungs, sway inside your chest like tits
in a housedress. Perhaps you're frying liver
which shrinks like your father getting older.
You still smell him breathing all over
your skin. He drank himself to death.

Now each woman you meet is a giant.
You'd crawl up their legs & never come down.
Even when you think you're big enough
to touch them, his voice flies from under
your throat & "I love you" comes out
a drunk whimper. All you can do
is breathe louder. You're speaking
to the back of your mouth. Finally,
you admit you know nothing
about sex & drown the urge slowly
like a fat bird in oil.

Still, those wings inside you.
At the hot stove all day you feel yourself
rising, the kids wrapping themselves
around your legs oh it's sexual
this nourishing food for the family
your father stumbling through the door
calling to you Honey I'm home.

At first, because "fathers" is in the plural, this poem purports to be
addressed to all males whose fathers are literally or figuratively dead.

This sense that the poem is addressed to a collective but delineated "you" with whom the poet wishes to establish communion is augmented by "Perhaps you're frying liver," which seems to argue that whatever you are doing, but especially if you are a male doing something traditionally feminine such as cooking and had a "big" father with a tritely macho manner, you will be apt to feel "more/ of a mother"; you may have a queasy consciousness of your own softness, of your anima, of the androgynous nature of your sexuality. Regardless of how plausible or not this general hypothesis is, it is presented arrestingly enough that most readers will provisionally accept it as true, without losing faith in the poem; they will read on, curious to see whether the poem will clarify their feelings toward their fathers. But they will be quickly disappointed. As the poem continues, the reader increasingly encounters propositions that, although they may be applicable to the author, the reader can apply neither to himself nor to his second-hand knowledge of male experience. I, for one, do not, either literally or figuratively, "still smell" my father "breathing all over" my "skin." My father did not, literally or figuratively, drink himself to death. The account of sexual intercourse that Ryan gives in the second stanza is not typical of my experience, and for Ryan to assert that it is destroys for me the believability of the poem. Finally, of course, it becomes apparent that most of the poem's content, far from being hypothetical, must be drawn directly from the author's personal life, that the poem is an autobiographical account of Ryan's unresolved and tormented feelings about his own father, and that Ryan's initial claim that the poem would typify the lives of the rest of us will not only go unfulfilled: from the outset, Ryan never intended to make good on it.

More than either of the two previous poems we have seen, this one is crippled by the blurred-you. Just how poignant, how genuinely moving the poem could be if it were for "*my* dead father," if it were advanced as autobiography, may be seen when the first-person pronoun is substituted for "you" in the second stanza:

> Now each woman I meet is a giant.
> I'd crawl up their legs and never come down.
> Even when I think I'm big enough
> to touch them, his voice flies from under
> my throat & "I love you" comes out
> a drunk whimper. All I can do
> is breathe louder. I'm speaking
> to the back of my mouth. Finally,
> I admit I know nothing
> about sex & drown the urge slowly
> like a fat bird in oil.

This is the earnestness of the best poetry, of a person taking himself more seriously than is comfortable for most of us. Given the poem's subject, the temptation facing Ryan to cover his tracks and to slip into the blurred-you is quite understandable, for the posture of the speaker in the passage above is anything but dignified; but stripped of disguises the passage is not only more moving than the official version: if anything, it is more beautiful.

Nevertheless, the success of Ryan's first stanza—of that part of the poem that is rhetorically consistent and where, by deploying the blurred-you, Ryan seems to be describing a set of hypothetical situations that somehow typify a certain type of male experience—suggests that in some rhetorical situations the blurred-you may be a necessary fixture, that it could enable a poem to succeed. Such poems are not easy to find. Stephen Dunn's "The Party to Which You Were Never Invited" is one of them:

THE PARTY TO WHICH YOU WERE NEVER INVITED

> You walk in,
> your clothes are dark and appropriate,

that ramrod in your spine
never more arrogant.
You speak and the women move
away from you as if your mouth
were a wound; the men see tombstones
in your smile.
They think they know who you are,
they think they can throw you out
as they could one man.
But you are every man who has ever
been omitted from any list, the vengeance
in just one of your arms
could destroy a city.
And they are right about your teeth
which are like the broken bones of children
not unlike theirs, but they are wrong
if they think the police
can stop a man who is thousands.
You pour yourself a drink,
cock your elbow as if ready to speak
the latest gossip.
By now, they are huddled in corners.
You have dreamed of this moment,
dreamed of a woman brave enough
to embrace you, someone wise enough
to know you could be ruined by kindness.
No one moves.
You start with the lamps, twisting them
indistinguishable from coat hangers.
You shake a man's hand until it's a little
white rubber glove,
and all the while the others are screaming,
unaware of how much you need them,
how much you would love them
if they knew how to stop you.

Why does the blurred-you work here and not in the other poems? First of all, the referent of "you" is not really "blurred." Throughout the poem "you" consistently carries the sense of "one," and Dunn leaves clear cues to this effect. The title is obviously shorthand for "*Any* Party to Which *One* Was Never Invited." The only reason for the definite article is to further cue the reader that, instead of presenting a collection of hypothetical revenge fantasies, Dunn intends to present one grand revenge fantasy as typical of the breed. The only reason for "you" instead of "one" is, as I have already mentioned, that "one" would sound unnecessarily stuffy. From the outset, then, Dunn is obviously advancing a proposition that is entirely hypothetical, and if there is any doubt about that, it is erased by the passage "But you are every man who has ever/ been omitted from any list. . . ." At every juncture the poem is saying, "*If* one were angry at being left out of a social gathering, this is the *kind* of fantasizing to which one might resort."

It is in poems like this one, where the entire poem is a hypothesis following an implicit injunction to "suppose. . . ," that the blurred-you is appropriate. Phil Dacey's witty poem, "The Obscene Caller," is set up this way. The poem opens:

> Years ago,
> he began dialing your number.
> He is still dialing.
> At the precise moment
> he finishes dialing,
> you will arrive home.
> He will sound
> as you might expect.
> For a moment
> you will think it could be
> your father. . . .

These lines are a shorthand for something like "Suppose that, years ago, he began dialing your number, that he is still dialing, but that, at the precise moment he finishes dialing, you arrive home so that, instead of his sounding as you might expect, for a moment you think it is your father. . . ." Here, as in the Dunn poem, the prefix "suppose" has been omitted to make the hypothesis more immediate, to tease the reader for a moment, inviting his suspension of disbelief, inviting him to play the game; but the title, combined with the hypothetical "you" and the far-fetched proposition of the first sentence, sufficiently cues the reader as to the rules of this game, and whatever doubt the reader has will be erased by the future tense: "you will arrive home."

Just how necessary the blurred-you is in the Dunn poem may be seen if we substitute first-person pronouns for the second-person pronouns. The substitution destroys the poem. It works against our sense of the poem as a hypothesis. If we were to read "I walk in,/ my clothes are dark and appropriate," we would assume that the poem was describing an actual revenge fantasy that the author had suffered instead of typifying the kind of fantasy he or any of us *might* have. At first, this does not seem seriously to hurt the poem, but, when we reach propositions such as "the men see tombstones in my smile" or "the vengeance in just one of my arms could destroy a city," we see more clearly why the poem must use the blurred-you. What Dunn intends to do is gently to make fun of the typical revenge fantasy, to parody it by exaggerating it, by making it deliberately melodramatic. In a tone both urbane and sardonic, he is criticizing it. He has to use "you" because, if the poem were written in the first person, the reader, believing he was reading a transcription of an actual fantasy by the author, would dismiss on logical grounds the element of parody, of deliberate exaggeration, and hence miss the whole point of the poem. How could the poem "exaggerate" or "parody" if it were an actual fantasy?

To recast Dunn's piece in the first person would not only destroy the logic of its position: it would also destroy the poem's tone. A proposition such as "my teeth . . . are like the broken bones of children" sounds too hysterical, too "earnest" to be an urbane fantasy about fantasy. The author must not, at any juncture, seem to forget himself or seem to be totally in earnest, or he will compromise the balance of sympathy and detachment that, like a tightrope walker, Dunn manages to maintain to the end. Whereas the earnestness of the first-person point of view is required by the decorum of serious testimony, the urbane, sardonic, detached pretense of sympathy that the blurred-you generates is more appropriate to the decorum of satire. Indeed, Dunn's posture throughout the poem is strikingly like that of a stand-up comedian facing a live audience. Although his poem is fairly effective on the printed page, it would be even more effective delivered to a live audience. It would be terrifically funny. In fact, most poems that deploy the blurred-you are far more effective when delivered by the poet in person to a live audience than when they are on the page. The physical presence of the audience in silent communion with the poet serves as a kind of confirmation of the pact that the blurred-you asserts because at every turn the mention of "you" is substantiated by the palpable sense of "us" that is endemic to the physical context of a reading. As a result, we no longer feel the poet straining when he says "you."

But whether or not the blurred-you is the most appropriate pronoun for a given poem (on the page or performed live) is another question entirely. To assess the effectiveness and propriety of the blurred-you in a poem being performed by its author before a live audience, we must consider elements of the performance, and here the distinction that Northrop Frye makes between "radicals of presentation"—between "lyric" and *epos*—is essential: In "lyric," the poet "normally pretends to be talking to himself or to some else. . . . The poet, so to speak, turns his back to his listeners. . . ."

In *epos*, "the radical of presentation is oral address. . . . *Epos* thus takes in all literature, in verse or prose, which makes some attempt to preserve the convention of recitation and a listening audience."[3]

Of the four poems we have seen, Dunn's is the only one that clearly intends to preserve "the convention of recitation and a listening audience." It is a mimesis of *epos*. The other poems are intended as lyric. They are intensely personal songs designed to be overheard, to be sung as though the poet were unaware of his audience. Since "you" acknowledges the presence of an audience, it is inappropraate to the lyric mode. The first three poems should be in the first person. This is not to say that they could not be effectively delivered at a poetry reading. Although the lyric mode is more effective on the page, where the audience is not in the physical presence of the poet so that the poet's song is truly overheard, the lyric radical is possible before a live audience, provided that, as he performs the poem, the poet affect total unawareness of the audience—a posture that is impossible when the blurred-you governs his poem. The three lyric poems will be most effective if transposed into the first person and if offered as literature, slightly less effective if performed properly before an audience. If they retain the blurred-you, they will be more effective delivered live than on the page, but in neither instance will they work as well as in the first-person singular, which, along with the second-person-singular pronoun, is the pronoun endemic to the lyric. Conversely, Dunn's poem, as it is written, will be most effective performed live. Its effect as literature is diminished, but still considerable. If transposed into the first-person singular, it becomes risky if performed live and reads like madness on the printed page.

Despite the institution of "the poetry reading," virtually all of the important poetry of the 1970s is intended first as literature, second as oral performance. For this reason alone, it is necessarily lyric; for the physical isolation of the author from the reader gives all his utterances an overheard quality such that, in order most effectively to exploit the reader's expectations, it is safest for a poet to imagine himself in the lyric radical—a radical that, because he is ostensibly alone, gives him the license to "go naked." Perhaps, as poets increasingly feel the limitations of a poetic based on testimony—the requirement to go naked—they are trying, through the blurred-you, to impart a more hypothetical—a "fictional"—epistemology to their poems, to insist on their prerogative to invent freely. Perhaps the misapplication of the blurred-you is the natural defense of the lyric poet who has to read frequently on the circuit, enabling him to deliver a lyric utterance before an audience without feeling quite so exposed. Or perhaps a heavy diet of live readings subtly changes a poet's sense of audience so that, half-consciously, he begins adapting his poetry for live performance: as he sits down to write, he finds himself thinking, "This will go over well." The fact remains, however, that poetry is literature first and oration second. To the extent that a poem does not acknowledge this fact, it will fail to achieve its maximum potential as literature.

Notes

1. *50 Contemporary Poets*, ed. Alberta T. Turner (New York: David McKay, 1977), p. 269.

2. Ibid., p. 270.

3. Northrop Frye, *Anatomy of Criticism* (Princeton: Princeton University Press, 1957), pp. 248–50.

Four

THE "PROSE LYRIC"

In his essay "Chapter and Verse," Stanley Plumly coined the pro-
vocative term "prose lyric" to refer to

> free verse . . . preoccupied with its own voice and rhetoric, the voice of the
> emotion, a voice tested by its ability to create and control tone. . . . the
> terms and means of fiction, as well as the larger rhythms and language of
> prose, help establish a forum for such poetry.[1]

Plumly traces the origins of the "prose lyric" back to the normalization of "free verse":

> What has happened in the seventies is that as free verse has become the
> norm, it has become more refined, more various, and more abused. At its
> flexible best, it calls less and less attention to the language and more to the
> body of the action. . . . As a genre of under a hundred lines, free verse has
> come to mean the dramatic lyric, an intensified, implicative action. What
> makes that action convincing or authentic is the tone of its master's voice.
> Tone is what we are left with once the language assumes transparency.
> . . . the intersection of the flexibility of the free verse rhythm with the
> strategy of storytelling has produced a kind of prose lyric: a form corrupt
> enough to speak flat out in sentences yet pure enough to sustain the inten-
> sity, if not the integrity of the line.[2]

The "prose lyric"—with all the best intentions, Plumly has, both in

"The 'Prose Lyric'" originally appeared in *The Ohio Review* and is reproduced here, with minor
changes, by permission.

this label and in his account of what lies behind it, been the only critic to face squarely the logical dead end posed by the current domination of American poetry by "free verse": the inevitable conclusion that what we regard as "poetry" has much more to do with the rhetorical expectations generated by a verse format than with any structural elements inherent in the "line."

The assumptions behind the term "prose lyric" are not, however, so new as they might seem. The notion of poetry as primarily a rhetorical convention is explicit in Northrop Frye's formulation of the lyric: "The lyric is . . . preeminently the utterance that is overheard."[3] And it is everywhere implicit in the New-Critical fuss about irony. Thirty years ago, when Cleanth Brooks in his essay "Irony and 'Ironic' Poetry" analyzed "Dover Beach," he was every bit as attentive to tone as Plumly is now:

> The speaker in "Dover Beach" states that the world . . . "Hath really neither joy nor love nor light. . . ." How can it [the truth of the statement] be validated? . . . when we raise such a question, we are driven to consider the poem as drama. We are forced to raise such further questions as these: Does the speaker seem carried away with his own emotions? Does he seem to oversimplify the situation? Or does he, on the other hand, seem to have won to a kind of detachment and objectivity? In other words, we are forced to raise the question as to whether the statement grows properly out of a context; whether it acknowledges the pressures of the context; whether it is "ironical"—or merely callow, glib, and sentimental.[4]

In the passage above, Brooks is not, of course, concerned with what a poem is but with practical criticism—with judging whether a poem sounds authentic or not. But implicit throughout his argument is his recognition of the crucial role of the rhetorical contract in generating emotion. Brooks sounds remarkably like Plumly when Plumly says:

> If the lyric is the fragment of our time, then tone is its authenticating means. The poet would convince us that the piece he is giving us is not from whole cloth but from the total fabric. Without the self-appointed skills the for-

malist can display, the free verse poet is especially vulnerable to questions of credentials. The tone of his voice, as it brings together what is happening with why it is happening, as it gives thought to the emotion, as it calls more and more attention to the person behind the performance, must pass some fairly tough tests as to what is true as well as what is beautiful.[5]

Paralleling this steadily growing critical recognition of the rhetorical basis of poetry is a growing uneasiness about the role of rhythm in poetry. Despite all the evidence to the contrary, however, the impulse behind most examinations of open-form prosody seems still to be to try to find some structural justification for "verse," some necessity, if not for meter, then for the line. For example, in his essay "The Line in Poetry," Miller Williams argues that "the line is the structural and functional unit of the printed poem, as decidedly as the paragraph is the unit of both structure and function in exposition," because, when a line "works," at the end of it "the reader feels rhythmically pleased but expectant."[6] Although Williams is right, it seems to me to be almost a defensive measure to devote an entire essay to pleading the existence of such a slight effect in verse. Has verse been reduced to *only* the dispositions of a few line breaks? There is something defensive, too, in Paul Fussell's interesting essay "Free Verse," where he adduces some examples of how "free-verse lines, deprived of pattern in one dimension, the metrical, tend to compensate by employing another kind of pattern, conspicuous repetition of phrases or syntactical forms."[7] The boldest and most thorough denial of the evidence is Harvey Gross's:

> The view I take is that meter, and prosody in general, is itself meaning. Rhythm is neither outside of a poem's meaning nor an ornament to it. Rhythmic structures are expressive forms . . . communicating those experiences which rhythmic consciousness can alone communicate.[8]

It would be nice if these attempts to justify free verse structurally could succeed; but the fact is that, when free verse, especially in the "plain style" that Mark Strand has said tries to "affect as much as possible the naturalness of conversation,"[9] has become so normalized that it no longer alludes to or plays itself off against metrical forms, when verse has become "prose" and no longer embodies the kind of rhythm Gross sees as endemic to poetry, its purported potential to communicate "those experiences which rhythmic consciousness can alone communicate" becomes only an assertion: its deployment serves only as a rhetorical gesture signifying its author's intention. Such a poem must rely almost entirely on rhetorical dispositions to render feeling. Consider, for example, Robert Bly's fine little piece, "Driving to Town Late to Mail a Letter":

> It is a cold and snowy night. The main street is deserted.
> The only things moving are swirls of snow.
> As I lift the mailbox door, I feel its cold iron.
> There is a privacy I love in this snowy night.
> Driving around, I will waste more time.

To appreciate fully the extent to which this poem fits the label "prose lyric," we might recall Gross's beguiling "definition" of a "poem":

> Our understanding of prosody's function is based on what a poem is, and how we conceive the nature of rhythm. . . . A poem is a symbol in which idea, experience, and attitude are transmuted into feelings; these feelings move in significant arrangements: rhythmically. It is prosody and its structures which articulate the movement of feeling in a poem, and render to our understanding meanings which are not paraphrasable.[10]

What Gross is asserting here is that poetry *is* "prosody." Yet the Bly poem simply lacks prosody. To be sure, its verse format alludes to prosody, but its cadence, like the rhythm of almost all of Bly's poetry, is leaden, clumsy, without the slightest relation to the poem's content. The poem has *no* rhythm. Nevertheless, the poem does, on a modest scale, "articulate the movement of feeling . . . and render to our understanding meanings which are not paraphrasable." It does so through rhetorical, rather than musical, artfulness.

The term "rhetorical" as I am using it here refers to the relation—the purported contract—between the speaker and his audience: the question of who is speaking to whom, through what mask, and for what ostensible purpose. The rhetorical artfulness of Bly's poem begins with his title, which posits the apparent occasion of the poem: what Bly experienced once when "Driving to Town Late to Mail a Letter." In the body of the poem, the conventional use of the present tense cues us that Bly is mentally re-enacting this occasion, pretending to talk to himself, yet intending to be "overheard." The middle three lines evoke, through imagery and word association, some of the recollected mood of that night. The last line, toward which the whole poem aims—a kind of fierce, exultant wink at the reader—plays off the title: "waste more time" resonates with "to Mail a Letter." Mailing a letter was never the real reason why the poet drove to town; it was an excuse to enjoy "the privacy . . . in this snowy night," an enjoyment that in Bly's mind is exhilarating and spiritually sustaining—anything but a waste of time. "Waste more time" thus has a kind of savage gaiety to it, an exuberance of irony that very accurately renders, to me at least, the giddy, pointless excitement we tend to feel when a big snow stops everything without inconveniencing us, leaves us with no obligations. The choice of "waste more time" instead of a less ironical phrase such as "take my time" is an adroit rhetorical move, effective because it slyly amends the initial rhetorical contract in order to surprise us. Not only does it reveal that the title is a deliberate deception; more important, it changes momentarily what Northrop Frye calls the poem's "radical of presentation." Until the poem's last three words, the radical of presentation is what Frye calls the lyric:

> The lyric poet normally pretends to be talking to himself or to someone else: a spirit of nature, a Muse . . . a personal friend, a lover, a god, a personified abstraction, or a natural object. . . . The poet, so to speak, turns his back on his listeners. . . .[11]

Were Bly to keep his back to his listeners all the way through the poem, he would end with something like "I will take more time." He would speak in his own dialect, as he does in the penultimate line. When he says "waste more time," Bly in effect half turns to the audience and says, "I will do what many of you would consider a waste of time." He acknowledges our presence. It is this sly violation by Bly of the poem's apparent radical of presentation that makes the ending so coy—a sort of challenge issued to the audience. Much of the poem's force depends on it. Just how subtle Bly's disclosure is may be seen if we imagine the poem with the same title but in the past tense:

> It was a cold and snowy night. The main street was deserted.
> The only things moving were swirls of snow.
> As I lifted the mailbox door, I felt its cold iron.
> There was a privacy I loved in that snowy night.
> Driving around, I wasted more time.

We get the point of this version easily enough, but somehow the force of the irony in "waste," the giggled challenge in it, is gone. Why? Because the poem's radical of presentation does not change at the end. Using the first person in the past tense, the speaker cannot pretend to be musing aloud, to be letting us eavesdrop. Instead, he faces us directly to narrate a story: the radical of presentation is now, to use Frye's terminology again, that of *epos*, which, as Frye puts it, "makes some attempt to preserve the convention of recitation and a listening audience."[12] The poem is similarly diminished if the third-person pronoun is substituted for the first-person pronoun while the present tense is kept. We get the point, but the poem does not, to use Gross's words, "render" so much "feeling." In short, then, we discover this paradox: The poem's ability to articulate a movement of feeling depends on a rhetorical consideration—manipulation of the radical of presentation—rather than on rhythm, even though we recognize the poem as a "lyric" and interpret the poem the same regardless of its pretended radical of presentation, that is, as an attempt to articulate a movement of feeling in the author—the person who signed his name to the verse.

In this respect Frye's notion of the "lyric" and Plumly's use of the term "lyric" have a great deal in common. Both Frye and Plumly envision "verse" when they use the term "lyric," but, more important, both regard verse as pre-eminently a rhetorical gesture rather than as a structural adaptation of language to function. To appreciate the way in which verse implies the convention of lyric, imagine the poem, with its title unchanged, printed as a prose poem:

> It is a cold and snowy night. The main street is deserted. The only things moving are swirls of snow. As I lift the mailbox door, I feel its cold iron. There is a privacy I love in this snowy night. Driving around, I will waste more time.

The prose format almost entirely obscures the poem's effect, so that it reads like the beginning of a story. "Driving around, I will waste more time" seems to anticipate merely another sentence such as "I stop at the deserted barber shop and look in," which in turn anticipates another sentence, part of a continuing narrative in which the poet, at loose ends, "wastes more time." In a verse format, convention requires that we pay special attention to the last line of a poem, that we regard it as a sort of musical finale: the resolution of a chord progression, the completion of a pattern, the conclusion of a process. If, to borrow again from Gross, a poem "articulates the movement of feeling," we expect, if not a climax, then some sense of a natural ending to this movement. True, the prose paragraph does, by convention, assert a certain degree of closure, and well-written paragraphs often end crisply, with a satisfying sense of finality. But this finality is usually not "lyrical," not the resolution of a complex movement of feeling that we expect at the end of some lines of verse. When we arrive at the end of the prose version of Bly's poem, we are preoccupied by narrative conventions—the question, Then what did he do?—rather than lyrical conventions—the question, What is he feeling at *this* point?

As the prose corruption of Bly's poem indicates, it is the very presence of verse that causes the reader: (1) to regard Bly's utterance not as a narrative but as an attempt by the author to articulate a movement of feeling and (2) to refer this "movement of feeling" to the author, to attribute to the poem the overheard quality that Frye requires. In other words, printed verse implies a mimesis of the lyric radical of presentation—a rhetorical contract in which the articulated movement of feeling can be more intense than that in prose, can in fact be the principal subject matter of the poem because the author is pretending to be off-guard, to voice emotion that he would not voice "in public," if facing his audience directly. We see also from the three verse versions of the Bly poem that, although the mimesis of *epos* may be deployed to achieve a local effect in a poem, in a post-Gutenberg literary culture, where verse is published in books, the radical of presentation called *epos* hardly ever applies. Only when the poet is in the physical presence of his audience is the distinction between *epos* and "lyric" conspicuous enough to warrant consideration as the basis for genre. Virtually all verse on the printed page today is lyric, so that, when applied to contemporary American poetry, the terms "verse," "lyric," and "poetry" are synonymous and refer to the same rhetorical gesture.

The lowest common denominator of poetry, then, is the rhetorical gesture that the very act of choosing verse over prose implies. Obviously, however, most of the best poetry, although it depends on this rhetorical convention far more heavily than is immediately obvious, relies on additional means by which to enhance its asserted "movement of feeling." As with the Bly poem, one can get a rough idea of the dgree to which a poem goes beyond the fundamental rhetorical contract of verse by imagining the poem as prose or—a subtler test—by altering the contract, by changing the predominant tense of a poem or its predominant point of view. If, as was the case with the Bly poem, the alteration weakens (or strengthens) the overall feeling of the poem without changing its fundamental character, then the poem's ability to generate that feeling is based mainly on the rhetorical strategy behind the "prose lyric." But if the alteration has a significant effect on the kind (rather than the degree) of feeling that the poem renders, then that feeling must stem from factors not merely rhetorical but inherent in the poem's structure. Consider, for example, the following passage from James Wright's *Two Citizens*, a passage whose prosody seems to contribute heavily to what William Matthews has so aptly called the poem's "exalted giddiness":[13]

> What have I got to do?
> The sky is shattering,
> The plain sky grows so blue.
> Some day I have to die,
> As everyone must do
> Alone, alone, alone,
> Peaceful as peaceful stone.
> You are the earth's body.
> I will die on the wing.
> To me, you are everything
> That matters, chickadee.
> You live so much in me.
> Chickadees sing in the snow.
> I will die on the wing,
> I love you so.

The most common-sense rhetorical considerations dictate that love poems be in the first-person singular, be addressed to the beloved or refer to the beloved in the third-person singular. To this extent, the Wright passage depends on a rhetorical disposition: the first-person point of view is an earnest of sincerity. But the power of

Wright's poem, regardless of its sincerity, seems to issue from a source that has little to do with point of view or with convention: the poem is so much better than the average prose lyric because most of its power flows from an energy *within* the language. Just how true this is may be seen if we commit the deliberate heresy of imagining the piece sung by Wright to a woman about how much another man loves her:

> What has he got to do?
> The sky is shattering,
> The plain sky grows so blue.
> Some day he has to die,
> As everyone must do
> Alone, alone, alone,
> Peaceful as peaceful stone.
> You are the earth's body.
> He will die on the wing.
> To him, you are everything
> That matters, chickadee.
> You live so much in him.
> Chickadees sing in the snow.
> He will die on the wing,
> He loves you so.

The result is as grotesque as it is precisely because, even with the minor changes in wording, there is so much power inherent in the poem's structure, so much feeling that, divorced from the first-person point of view, the emotion clearly exceeds the requirements of the dramatic occasion, so that the poem sounds mawkish, pathetic, voyeuristic, hysterical—the half-sobbed sentimental effusion of a man vicariously caught up in somebody else's romance. The quantity of emotion that the corrupted version generates remains roughly the same, but its quality does not. If we were to put the original

Wright passage into prose, we would see an analogous effect. Whereas our temptation with the prose version of the Bly poem was merely to read it as narrative, with the Wright passage we would be struck simply by the impropriety of the prose frame to such language.

The dependence of the Wright poem on structure, however, is only a measure of its quality. If we were to claim that the Wright poem is true poetry whereas the Bly poem is not, we would not only be slighting the lesser but still evident merits of the Bly poem; we would also be using the term "poetry" honorifically, as critics from Wordsworth and Coleridge on have too often used it: to refer to the kind of verse that they endorse. When applied to contemporary American poetry, the term "poetry" should be regarded as synonymous with the term "lyric," which is simply another word for the rhetorical convention signaled by "verse."

It is the equivalence of "poetry" to "lyric" to "verse" that is the basis for the "prose lyric," the poetry of our moment—a poetry of sensibility because the dramatic context of the prose lyric, however obliquely, always refers to the same ultimate source, the author; a poetry particularly well adapted to the mass production of poets by university writing programs because, as Plumly implies, to produce a decent facsimile of a prose lyric requires minimum credentials. One does not need a fine ear or a deep familiarity with tradition. Any bright student, once having studied a few of the better forums where the prose lyric is published and once having grasped the rhetorical principle behind free verse and the current rules of decorum, which require that a poem affect a certain degree of spontaneity— enough to make it sound, as Albert Goldbarth puts it, "earned and urgent"—could turn out passable specimens of the mode within a week. The poetry that will survive us, however, will always be more than rhetorical. Whether the open-form verse of James Wright's later pieces or the strict prosody of Theodore Roethke's "My Papa's Waltz," its painfully forged yet inexplicable music will have an immediate authority that we will heed whether we want to or not and that we will remember for the rest of our lives.

Notes

1. Stanley Plumly, "Chapter and Verse: Part II," *American Poetry Review* 7 (May-June 1978): 21.

2. Stanley Plumly, "Chapter and Verse," *American Poetry Review* 7 (January-February 1978): 23, 27.

3. Northrop Frye, *Anatomy of Criticism* (Princeton: Princeton University Press, 1957), p. 249.

4. Cleanth Brooks, "Irony and 'Ironic' Poetry," *College English* 9 (February 1948): 233–34.

5. Plumly, "Chapter and Verse," *American Poetry Review* 7 (January-February 1978): 23.

6. Miller Williams, "The Line in Poetry," *Antaeus* 30/31 (Summer/Autumn): 309.

7. Paul Fussell, "Free Verse," *Antaeus* 30/31 (Summer/Autumn): 299.

8. Harvey Gross, *Sound and Form in Modern Poetry* (Ann Arbor: University of Michigan Press, 1968), p. 12.

9. "A Conversation with Mark Strand," *Ohio Review* 13 (Winter 1972): 58.

10. Gross, p. 10.

11. Frye, p. 249.

12. Ibid., p. 248.

13. William Matthews, "The Continuity of James Wright's Poems," *Ohio Review* 18 (Spring–Summer 1977): 56.

Five

STEPHEN DUNN
AND THE REALIST LYRIC

In his first three collections, Stephen Dunn has succeeded in what may be the most difficult task facing an American poet today: he has somehow managed to transform the most unpromising and subtly demeaning material—a frank and realistic account of the banalities of middle-class American life—into art of the highest caliber without satirizing that material, without placing himself above it or outside it, without blurring the distinction between fantasy and reality, even while admitting the degree to which fantasy and daydream figure in his own quotidian experience.

The obstacles that any serious writer, novelist or poet, faces when trying to treat that material in a realist mode are almost insuperable. For reasons Christopher Lasch has suggested, the temptation facing a writer to adopt the urbane, post-modernist mode of a Kurt Vonnegut or a Donald Barthelme is almost irresistible:

> While modern industry condemns people to jobs that insult their intelligence, the mass culture of romantic escape fills their heads with visions of experience beyond their means—beyond their emotional and imaginative capacities as well—and thus contributes to a further devaluation of routine. The disparity between romance and reality, the world of the beautiful people and the workaday world, gives rise to an ironic detachment that dulls pain but also cripples the will to change social conditions. . . .

> Escape through irony and critical self-awareness is in any case itself an illusion; at best it provides only momentary relief. Distancing soon becomes a routine in its own right. Awareness commenting on awareness creates an escalating cycle of self-consciousness. . . .
>
> As for art, it not only fails to create the illusion of reality but suffers from the same crisis of self-consciousness that afflicts the man in the street. . . . By means of irony and eclecticism, the writer withdraws from his subject but at the same time becomes so conscious of these distancing techniques that he finds it more and more difficult to write about anything but the difficulty of writing. Writing about writing then becomes in itself an object of self-parody. . . .[1]

The theme of "the disparity between romance and reality" has, of course, been treated seriously and beautifully in prose fiction. Of all the novels dealing with it, Walker Percy's *The Moviegoer* is perhaps the best because it manages to condescend neither to Binx nor to "the movies." Percy does not, as Lasch would phrase it, "withdraw from his subject." But, with the exception of a few, our current novelists claim immunity from the daydreams afflicting their characters. For example, Barthelme's pieces, while they acknowledge in their very texture the pervasiveness of daydream in our lives, refuse to abandon the safe, noncommittal vantage point of irony, of parody. As Lasch puts it, while indicting Vonnegut as typical of most "experimental" authors:

> By fogging over the distinction between truth and illusion, he asks the reader to believe his story not because it rings true or even because he claims it conceivably might be true—at least in part—if the reader chose to believe him. The writer waives the right to be taken seriously, at the same time escaping the responsibilities that go with being taken seriously. He asks the reader not for understanding but indulgence.[2]

The very factors that tempt the fiction writer to effect, by "fogging over the distinction between truth and illusion," a chic postmodernist withdrawal, confront the poet with a threat that, though analogous, is rather more serious. The poet's subject matter is apt to seem limited—so much so that in what Lasch calls "the workaday world" of the 1970s, perhaps ninety-five percent of a person's daily experience is virtually unavailable for poetry. The reason it is so is almost entirely conventional. Poets are traditionally thought to be people of vision and purity, who manage to live more intensely and richly than the general run of mankind. As Wordsworth put it, the poet is presumed to have a "more comprehensive soul" than is "common among mankind." Such a soul, we should suppose, would never take seriously such diversions as television. Novelists, on the other hand, have always had a tacit license to lower themselves to experience lives lesser than their own. As W. H. Auden puts it in "The Novelist":

> . . . to achieve his lightest wish, he must
> Become the whole of boredom, subject to
> Vulgar complaints like love, among the Just
>
> Be just, among the Filthy filthy too,
> And in his own weak person, if he can,
> Must suffer dully all the wrongs of Man.

It could be argued, of course, that television experience is as "real" as any other experience, and in a sense it is: when watching television or daydreaming, we are experiencing something. But there is an obvious difference between watching a tennis match on television and playing tennis. When one watches television, one suspends activity and stops "living" in order to participate imaginatively in other people's lives. Such vicarious participation costs nothing. It exercises neither the body nor the mind. It entails no risk. It leaves one unchanged. When one plays tennis, on the other hand, one does so wholly to the exlusion of the other "lives" one could imagine, and the activity leaves one, at the very least, mentally and physically sweaty. To a considerable extent, then, it is true that life actually "lived" and life vicariously experienced through television and daydream are mutually exclusive so that we are justified in referring, as I do henceforth, to life experienced vicariously as "unlived" life and to first-hand experience as "lived" life.[3]

Traditionally, it has been assumed that lived life has greater value than unlived life. We admire heroes because their share of lived life seems to be greater than normal. But nowhere is this bias in favor of the lived life greater than in our expectations regarding poetry. Since the Romantics, virtually all English-language poetry in which the poet's sensibility is given a central position in the poem—poetry that might roughly be labelled "lyric"—tends to celebrate the capacity of the sensibility to intensify contact with the lived life, to bring the reader closer to the actual world, that he may experience it freshly, feel it more keenly. Such poetry still tends to be pastoral, perhaps because, since Wordsworth, a pastoral setting has come to serve as a sort of testament to the poet's immersion in the Actual (personified by Nature). In his "Preface," Wordsworth clearly identified the pastoral with the lived life and maintained that a poet requires it:

> Humble and rustic life was generally chosen, because, in that condition, the essential passions of the heart find a better soil in which they can attain their maturity . . . and speak a plainer and more emphatic language; because in that condition of life our elementary feelings . . . may be more accurately contemplated and more forcibly communicated; . . . because the passions of men are incorporated with the beautiful and permanent forms of nature.

Implicit in the passage above are the notions that poets should write about first-hand experience and that more of it seems to be available in a rural setting than in cities. Urban life and mass culture, according to Wordsworth, tend "to blunt the discriminating powers of the mind, and, unfitting it for all voluntary exertion, to reduce it to a state of almost savage torpor":

> The most effective of these causes are the great national events which are daily taking place, and the increasing accumulation of men in cities, where the uniformity of their occupations produces a craving for extraordinary in-

cident, which the rapid communication of intelligence hourly gratifies. To this tendency of life and manners the literature and theatrical exhibitions of the country have conformed themselves.

Wordsworth might have been referring to televised soap operas and professional football. So lasting has been the convention of associating the rural with the first-hand and the urban with the vicarious, so enduring as been the convention of requiring of the "lyric" poet testimony about the quality of his life, that even today, when most Americans live in cities, the best American poetry in the Romantic tradition—the work of poets such as Robert Bly, James Dickey, Galway Kinnell, Theodore Roethke, William Stafford and James Wright—is apt to be pastoral. Louis Simpson describes this convention succinctly, if a bit sarcastically, when he writes:

> To read some American poets, you would think they lived far away from roads and supermarkets, that they never had the thoughts of the people you meet, that they looked with the eyes of the crow and listened with the ears of the beaver. That their habitation was darkness and their house made of earth and stones. That they were pure in thought and deed.[4]

A good example of a contemporary poem in this tradition is Dickey's "In the Mountain Tent," which begins:

> I am hearing the shape of the rain
> Take the shape of the tent and believe it,
> Laying down all around where I lie
> A profound, unspeakable law.
> I obey, and am free-falling slowly
>
> Through the thought-out leaves of the wood
> Into the minds of animals.
> I am there in the shining of water
> Like dark, like light, out of Heaven.

Through his imagination, the speaker is approaching closer contact with nature. Although he is physically stationary, the process he is describing is an active one; he is making something happen, and it is having a palpable effect upon him, changing him, until

> As I wait as if recently killed,
> Receptive, fragile, half-smiling,
> My brow watermarked with the mark
> On the wing of a moth
>
> ....
>
> From holes in the ground comes my voice
> In the God-silenced tongue of the beasts.
> "I shall rise from the dead," I am saying.

The poet's intimate identification with natural process has led to a powerful revelation, one which appears to have left him permanently changed. Similarly, Kinnell's lyrics, particularly in his collection *The Book of Nightmares*, assume that "song" comes from immersion—often terrifying and dangerous immersion—in lived life. As the end of "Another Night in the Ruins" says:

> How many nights must it take
> one such as me to learn
> that we aren't, after all, made
> from that bird which flies out of its ashes,
> that for a man
> as he goes up in flames, his one work
> is
> to open himself, to *be*
> the flames?

The neo-surrealist mode in which poets such as Bly often operate is a disguised form of the same convention. Archetypal imagery serves as the poet's testament of his perception of a reality more fundamental than the one we are accustomed to. No wonder, then, that poets find it so difficult to write with much relish about television, daydream, or any form of unlived life. To do so is to risk impugning their own credentials as poets. So strong is the stigma of television that, even when our poets do write about it, they treat it with surgical gloves, with an Olympian detachment. For example, in his sonnet sequence, "Watching Football on T.V.," Howard Nemerov is careful never to imply that he himself watches football on television for any purpose other than to consider, from an anthropological perspective, the general meaning of it. The first few lines of the first sonnet make it abundantly clear that not Nemerov but other "people" watch pro football seriously:

> It used to be only Sunday afternoons,
> But people have got more devoted now
> And maybe three four times a week retire
> To their gloomy living room to sit before
> The polished box alive with silver light. . . .

Even in these opening lines—especially in the second line—one discovers a hint of mockery, a mockery that turns the lush imagery of "polished box alive with silver light" back on itself. The repugnant theme of television simply enhances the contradiction that runs throughout this kind of neo-classicism: a desire to build something beautiful, undercut by total disenchantment. Whether affecting folksiness, lyricism, or philosophical gravity, Nemerov always comes off sounding slightly cynical. But his difficulties epitomize the very real test faced by a contemporary American poet trying to write about unlived life. The poet is tempted to put himself above the material, to diminish it, to satirize it. This is fine, provided that the poet will settle for satire; but it is impossible to write a moving or a poignant lyric about material toward which one condescends or which one regards as ugly and trivial.

The poet Larry Levis expresses the problem beautifully:

> In fact, the landscapes I choose for my poems, often, have nothing to do with the landscape that surrounds me: when I look out my window I see my neighborhood, and I know that beyond it is a small, midwestern university town. . . . By this I mean the shopping mall, the suburbs, the business loops, the freeways and boutiques with cute names. They are all part of a modern reality that I would prefer to forget, or ignore.[5]

Levis says of this landscape: "I find that I have very little desire to write anything about it" because, "to confront this reality without a context, without the possibility of a romance, is, as Stevens phrases it, 'to confront fact in its total bleakness.'" It is hardly surprising when Levis admits, "My most frequent problem as a poet is to have no subject, to have 'nothing at heart.'"[6]

In his frank and admirable statement, Levis reveals what is perhaps the greatest temptation facing the contemporary poet. Whereas the temptation facing the fiction writer is, as we have seen, to avoid making value judgments of the world, to spin post-modernist narratives that maintain ironic distance by fogging over the distinction between truth and fiction, the temptation facing the poet, if he is to avoid sounding cranky and cynical, is simply to limit his subject matter, to avoid writing about the difficult subjects, the boutiques, the malls, television, daydream, and whatnot. The poetry that results from that kind of withdrawal is, like the poetry of such writers as Dickey, Kinnell, Bly, Stafford, and Maxine Kumin, extremely beautiful, poetry none of us would want to do without; but compared to the tougher poems of writers such as David Ignatow, Louis Simpson, and, of course, Stephen Dunn—poems that tackle the ugliest and most sterile terrain—it is *easy* poetry.

Nevertheless, as the following poem from Dunn's third collection, *A Circus of Needs* (1978), indicates, it is possible to write seriously and feelingly about a television experience—about one's sense of unlived life— without sounding cynical or crabby or silly:

THE WEATHERMAN

Tonight I've decided to tell you, friends,
how much bad weather excites me.
I love the way it moves
state to state, and though I seem to rejoice
when it blows out to sea, that's just showbiz,
I'd like it to perch off the Carolinas
or double back across the nation,
and I know some of you feel the same.
Something in me responds to a low
and I'm sorry, I can watch the footage
from tornado damage all evening.
I know you too like to see cars off the road,
families disconnected, I know when you sigh
and say "How sad" your heart is thumping
to a tune you hardly understand. Friends,
this is a communication tonight,
not a broadcast. Here in the East
where no weather originates, where everything
moves toward us and so little arrives;
here, where we're forced to watch things
break up, or swerve toward Erie, what is it
that has turned in us, that has turned in me?
All I know is I can't deny the secret
happiness when a system moves across Nebraska
as I thought it would, paralyzing North Platte,
the National Guard called out, wind chill
(just the words *wind chill*) plunging
into my imagination. And you who live out there
where weather is a fact of life, don't you
secretly love it and look forward to it,
don't you love to survive it? And I mean *love*.
When I lived in Minnesota half my life
was the weather. A blizzard was me

and the blizzard. A tornado meant
the southwest corner of my basement
huddled with loved ones. Never have I been
so happy. It is we in the East I worry about;
only in August when the hurricanes wend up
from the Bahamas are our bodies truly connected
to our minds. Only then can devastation
make our lives less academic, only then
can we trace a path that leads directly
to ourselves. . . .

From this point, the poem becomes a bit redundant and perhaps
goes on longer than necessary. But on the whole this is a genuinely
poignant poem, even a beautiful one, because it manages to avoid
taking cheap shots: it refuses to condescend to its subject matter—
television and daydream. The main reason why it works is its mask.
By letting the weatherman seem to be speaking instead of himself,
Dunn is able to organize all his aimless fantasies into one solemn
and ceremonial broadcast. It is a rhetoric *trouvé*, but it is ideal for
Dunn's purposes because, by playing off the confession—the anarchic and gleeful secrets of the inner life—against the pompous and
brittle veneer of the broadcast format, he can measure accurately, in
every sentence, the grotesque discrepancy between the external public decorum of official life and the lawlessness of the inner life, with
all its impractical cravings and subversive fancies. More important,
however, the mask provides Dunn with a rhetorical stance from
which he can speak frankly about his weather fantasies without
breathing in our faces. It allows Dunn a certain obliquity, a tactful
way to confess.

At first glance, Dunn's posture in this poem, as in a good per-
centage of his poems, is something like that of a stand-up comedian.
The poem resembles a routine, a gag, with the comedian mimicking
another voice. But there is a crucial difference between this routine

and stand-up comedy. Everything this weatherman says is poignantly true, perfectly honest, with very little exaggeration. There is no silliness, no slapstick. This weatherman is not being held up for ridicule. He is not being parodied or satirized. Why is it, then, that what he is saying no professional weatherman would ever voice on the air? Obviously, because the voice speaking the poem is the voice of a weatherman saying what Dunn wishes weathermen would say—that is, what Dunn thinks as he watches the weather. It is, in fact, Dunn speaking all along, about how, bored with dailiness, we crave to have adventure imposed on us by one of the few aspects of our environment that we are unable to control: the weather.

Hence the poem is lyrical—the voice of a single man musing to himself, aware that the process of his inner life is being overheard. It is an accomplishment that, until I encountered Dunn's poetry, I had been convinced was impossible: a serious lyric poem based directly on television experience, a poem that violates at every turn traditional lyric decorum. It does not purport to testify on behalf of Dunn's special sensibility. It does not trace the story of an intensified moment of living, culminating in some extraordinary revelation that leaves the poet changed. Nothing happens. The poet is left unchanged. The poem is about how, in our lives, most of the time nothing happens. The poem is only a daydream—quite a plausible one—yet it is dramatic—the drama of life as it mostly is, the findings of a poet who, like Auden's novelist, in order to speak the truth is willing to "become the whole of boredom" if necessary, to appear "in his own weak person."

Of all Dunn's themes, the most daring is a description of the unlived life—where it sits in relation to lived life and what its uses are. Although Dunn prefers lived life, he is too honest to ignore such a large proportion of our experience as the unlived life. He insists on giving it equal time, and he tries to write about it realistically. The opening poem of Dunn's first collection, *Looking for Holes in the Ceiling* (1974), announces these intentions. This poem, "What," is a kind of *ars poetica*:

> What starts things
>
> are the accidents behind the eyes
> touched off by, say, the missing cheekbone
> of a woman who might have been beautiful
>
> it is thinking about
> your transplanted life-line going places
> in someone else's palm, or the suicidal games
> your mind plays with the edge
> of old wounds. . . .
>
> there are no endings
>
> . . . .
>
> what stops things for a moment
> are the words you've found for the last bit of light
> you think there is

The "accident" of "the missing cheekbone" suggests an impulse to fantasize beauty—the ideal—when it is not present. The possibility of a "transplanted life-line" suggests an impulse to daydream about oneself leading a life different from one's present life. The phrase "might have been" in line three echoes throughout the rest of the piece. What activates the imagination, what impels Dunn to write is apt to be the might-have-been rather than what is. "There are no endings" suggests that, in the world unredeemed by daydream, situations are never resolved patly as they often are in fantasy. "The last bit of light" is any light, be it imagined or real. "Light" is so temporary that, regardless of its quality, it is all worth salvaging by "words."

In the same collection, Dunn's "Carrying On" deliberately echoes "What":

> Here, on the landscape between wishes
> and preposterous conclusions, leaves
> early in October anticipate their own death
>   and rainbows
> sometimes appear in the sky like smiles
> from men who've just exercised their power.
> ....
>   I want to write
> notes to eleven-year-old girls who might
>   grow up
> to love me. I want to ask madmen why I feel
> if I were to walk into an opening anywhere
> the bones in my nose would be crushed
>   by the invisible glass.
> I don't.   I return to what's around me, birds
> that seem too nervous to fly, rocks
> as aimless as lost knuckles. . . .
> ....
>   . . . I dash off
> a dozen wry, complex sentences
> to the unattainable this, the unattainable that,
>   . . . It works;
>   for days I'm able
> to pull rabbits out of the thinnest afternoons.
> And move. And write. And keep it going
> until it stops.

The first fancies that Dunn adduces—our tendency to humanize na-ture—consist of conventional literary personifications given an original turn. They even have a certain plausibility. But as Dunn keeps listing the kinds of daydreams to which he is prone, they become increasingly dangerous so that they scare even him. Why is it, he asks, that one can imagine things so vividly that they seem virtually to have "happened"? Are we all "madmen"? What is the relation between the anarchic, subversive inner life and "what's around me"? It is, he concludes, "complex"; moreover, it keeps things going, keeps things interesting, enables him to "pull rabbits out of the thinnest afternoon."

"To pull rabbits out of the thinnest afternoons"—the metaphor may be interpreted as "to write poems in spite of the dearth of interesting material," in spite of the thinness—the dull flavor, the diluted quality—of daily life, in which almost everything one really wants seems "unattainable." Dunn is the only poet I know of who actually writes about the problem of having too little to write about, a possibility that, because it may be true, is so intimidating to the middle-class poet that either it is glibly sidestepped by the trite but wholly false retort that "a good poet can write a good poem about anything" or it is simply not discussed.

In "Carrying On" this theme is explicit; in other Dunn poems it is not. Instead, an entire poem may act it out implicitly, as, for example, does "Monologue on the Way Out," which begins:

> I've been to places where the laughter is as contagious
>   as a yawn.
> I've been through windows, and other ordeals.
> ....
>
>
> ....
>
> Let's just say I know what rugs think of the housewives who shake
> the footsteps from them, and call it cleaning.
> Let's just say I know why midgets think of buying horses
> and killing themselves in parks that have no statues.

The entire poem is structured as a catalogue, a list of false starts, of possible beginnings for poems, none of which gets off the ground. The poem ends wearily: "Let's just say I've been people who knew these things." Nothing has happened. None of the starts has generated a poem. But, paradoxically, when placed all together, they constitute a poem about the inability to find a subject for a poem.

Dunn's poems may be sorted thematically into four rough categories: There are poems such as the two above, in which not even rabbits can be pulled from the afternoon, which act out the process of coming to nothing. There are eloquent poems such as "Carrying On" about the *need* for rabbits. There are, of course, poems—many of Dunn's best—about lived life. And there are poems such as "The Weatherman," in which Dunn will take a typical middle-class fantasy and give it full play. Those of the fourth category are Dunn's most radical poems because they run squarely against the conventions of post-Romantic lyric, break new ground. One such poem, also in *Looking for Holes in the Ceiling*, is "Dancing on Park Avenue":

> It doesn't matter,
> but when the sun comes up
> who can say I didn't bring it?
> I am dancing on Park Avenue.
>
> A man closes his lids
> on my entire body.
> Taxi drivers scream
> "Faggot" through their side vents.
>
> The woman in me is ecstatic.
> She has never heard such praise.
> "Fruit!" someone else yells;
> I have kept her hidden too long.
>
> There are no words that can touch
> my manhood. I am the cock

of the sleeping fifties,
doing the flamenco.

I have attracted a small crowd.
I ask them, who can separate the dancer
from the dance?   They are calling the police
in their heads.   I ask them to reach out

for the missing rib of their existence.
I ask them for their bodies,
for the beautiful numbed beast
of their childhood. They are

silent. They are not really here.
The wind is blowing empty cartons
down the street.
I put away my breasts

and walk home dodging cracks
in the sidewalk.
It is still dark.
No one is awake.

Beyond the observation that the last two lines of this piece have an
obvious double meaning, implying that modern American culture
is still in the "dark" ages in its compartmentalized concepts of sexual
identity, the poem requires little comment. It is another Dunn
poem in which much is desired but in which nothing happens. The
poem compels us to take that condition seriously. What rescues the
poem from being comical are the harshly realistic reminders of how
endangered the inner life would be if uncaged: "Taxi drivers scream/
'Faggot' through their side vents." What rescues the poem from
sounding sick are its moments of deliberate but modulated self-par-
ody in lines such as "I ask them, who can separate the dancer/ from

the dance?" and "I am the cock/ of the sleeping fifties,/ doing the flamenco." The final synthesis of Dunn's attitudes toward his fantasy is complex and realistic. The poem takes the fantasy seriously— treats it as an experience as important as any part of lived life—even while recognizing the limitations and dangers of this type of "experience." The validation of such experience is clinched by the poem's beautiful ending, which evinces a genuine grief that nothing has happened—the kind of disappointment we feel when we are jolted from an afternoon nap, out of the warm lining of a dream. The poem is a realistic poem about a fantasy.

Another such piece in *Looking for Holes in the Ceiling* is "On Hearing the Airline Will Use a Psychological Profile to Catch Potential Skyjackers":

> They will catch me
> as sure as the check-out girls
> in every Woolworths have caught me, the badge
> of my imagined theft shining in their eyes.
>
> I will be approaching the ticket counter
> and knowing myself, myselves,
> will effect [*sic*] the nonchalance of a baron.
> That is what they'll be looking for.
>
> I'll say "Certainly is nice that the
> airlines are taking these precautions,"
> and the man behind the counter
> will press a secret button,
>
> there'll be a hand on my shoulder
> (this will have happened before in a dream),
> and in a back room they'll ask me
> "Why were you going to do it?"

I'll say "You wouldn't believe
I just wanted to get to Cleveland?"
"No," they'll say.
So I'll tell them everything,

the plot to get the Pulitzer Prize
in exchange for the airplane,
the bomb in my pencil,
heroin in the heel of my boot.

....

And on and on, celebrating myself, offering
no resistance, assuming what they assume,
knowing, in a sense, there is no such thing
as the wrong man.

This poem exemplifies well Dunn's extraordinary rhetorical sophistication. Like "Dancing on Park Avenue," the poem is totally realistic—probably everybody, whether guilty or innocent, who has passed through a security check of any kind has, simply because of the threat to his liberty, entertained subversive fantasies or suddenly realized that almost every element of his inner life *is* subversive—but how does one dramatize this banality, this faint odor of paranoia that is part of the weather of the American psyche, without taking any cheap shots, without being content with a trite, easy put-down? Dunn manages it by the adeptness with which he frames the poem. Just how adept may be seen if we imagine the poem with a different title, say, "Airport Security." Such a title would transform the piece into a tiresome Kafkaesque parable of an innocent man caught in the nightmare of a police state. We would be asked to imagine the events of the poem as a supposedly plausible hypothesis. But the title begins "On Hearing." These words should cue us that the poem is describing an event Dunn knows full well will never come to pass.

It is a nonevent that, out of a sort of nervous tic of the psyche, Dunn cannot prevent from nagging his imagination; hence the poem is about the act of imagining the event rather than the actual possibility of the event. It is about the inner life, its anarchic quality, its potential lawlessness. It is a realistic treatment of daydream. The hint that the narrative is not intended to describe a real possibility is clinched in the poem's first stanza, by the words "imagined theft." The gist of the first stanza, crudely paraphrased, says something like "It is a sure thing that, whenever I am in a situation where people suspect somebody of a crime, I will imagine that they think I am the guilty one, regardless of how innocent I act or how innocent my rational mind tells me I am." One of the best lines in the poem, comical because of its absurd accuracy, is the simple "'No,' they'll say." It captures perfectly the wooden rigidity of offical life when confronted with the charming logic of daydream. In the eyes of such obdurate stupidity and literal-mindedness, anything we say can be held against us. Tonally, the ending of this poem is just right. The speaker throws up his hands with a grim, amused resignation. It is serious without being shrill.

Although Dunn's poems about unlived life are his most important, his best poems are generally about lived life. In *Looking for Holes in the Ceiling*, "Day and Night Handball" may be the strongest (though perhaps the least intricate) piece, as good a sports poem as one can find. The poems in the book's center section, titled "Sympathetic Magic," also deal with lived life, but every one of these poems is in the instructional format. Dunn has perfect control of this rhetorical frame, and his results are subtle; however, the instructional format wears thin fast. Consider, for example, "Chipping Away at Death":

> Build a man of straw and rags
> and give him a foolish, battered hat.
> There, he is you in old age.

Then when the swallows come
from the south, dig up the brandy
you buried the year before.
Taste it. It will taste like
the musk of a religion
you gave up
for the sweeter taste of women.
Cover your straw man with it.
Light a match.
If you want to throw chestnuts
into the fire and sing
squalid songs as he burns, do so.
You are making sure none of this
will ever happen,
making sure this is one death
you will not suffer.

The instructional format is here a gimmick that enables the writer to give a slight turn to the ordinary so that we will notice it freshly. The poem advises us that, in order to "chip away" at death, we should try to imagine ourselves in old age and that when spring comes we should indulge in the delights of the world until we have forgotten all about that "straw man." Of course, Dunn knows that these are activities we all do anyhow—we do not need instructions— and that there is no way to avoid death. By pretending to instruct us in things that will be of absolutely no help and that we all do automatically, he hits us from ambush, as the full redundancy—the wry, hopeless irony—of his "instructions" dawns on us. The trick is elegant, but once we are alert to it, it loses most of its force. Dunn's best poems about lived life are direct. Like "Day and Night Hand- ball," like most poems that describe intense moments of lived life, they need not be rhetorically fancy. They can ride the cadence and the texture and the emotion of deeply lived experience:

I think of corner shots, the ball
hitting and dying like a butterfly
on a windshield, shots so fine
and perverse they begin to live

alongside weekends of sex
in your memory. I think of serves
delivered deep to the left hand,
the ball sliding off the side wall

into the blindnesses of one's body,
and diving returns that are impossible
except on days when your body is all
rubber bands and dreams

unfulfilled since childhood.
I think of a hand slicing the face
of a ball, so much english
that it comes back drunk

to your opponent who doesn't have
enough hands to hit it,
who hits it anyway, who makes you think
of "God!" and "Goddamn!", the pleasure

of falling to your knees
for what is superb, better than you.
....

....

Of Dunn's three collections so far, the second, *Full of Lust and
Good Usage* (1976), is his strongest. Most of the poems in the book's
first section are set in Marshall, Minnesota, where Dunn taught for
a while at Southwest Minnesota State College, in a "small town"

where "You begin to wish Barcelona would come/ to your town to live./ You wish Sophia Loren would place her/ finger on a knot you are tying," and where "the stars offer nothing after a while/ and nothing rises here, not even crime,/ during a full moon." So blandly wholesome is the surface of life there that it sometimes seems to Dunn as if

> no one anymore has any business
> by himself, or can go out to hear
> the changing edges of the wind, or watch
> one by one the lights go off in houses,
>
> without being strange. Say you made it known
> you had always been interested in
> how the darkness gets larger
> in your own town. Who would understand?

In such a literal environment, daydream and fantasy prove a kind of necessary inner resource:

> Your imagination is the only sure thing
>
> behind those windows. Stop worrying.
> Choose the most interesting word you can live with.
> Stick it on your forehead, publish it in
> the local paper. Say you won't let it down.

In perhaps the best poem in the first section, "Truck Stop: Minnesota," Dunn poignantly and candidly muses aloud on his feelings of alienation from middle America and on the comfort of fantasy as he watches a waitress in a truckstop:

> . . . Her face [has]
> the indecency of a billboard.
> She is the America I would like to love.

Sweetheart, the truckers call her.
Honey. Doll.
For each of them, she smiles.
I envy them,
I'm full of lust and good usage,
lost here.
I imagine every man she's left with
has smelled of familiar food,
has peppered her with wild slang
until she was damp and loose.
I do nothing but ask for a check
and drift out into the night air—
let my dreams lift
her tired feet off the ground
into the sweet, inarticulate
democracy beyond my ears—
and keep moving until I'm home
in the middle of my country.

What a hauntingly accurate and honest admission: one can feel so
"lost here" in America that it is only after he is back in his car safely
moving again, out of direct contact with the place—only when his
imagination, his "dreams" have "lifted" things to a more romantic
plane and softened them until a waitress is transformed into a wist-
ful symbol of "the America I would like to love"—only after he has
been lulled by the insulation of motion and fantasy on the highway
can he begin to feel at ease, at "home/ in the middle of my country."

Against this restless sense of too much life unlived, a feeling that
runs through the book's first section, is its second section, consisting
mainly of love poems about a honeymoon (or some highly erotic
vacation) in Nova Scotia. Most of these poems, like "Day and Night
Handball," are charged with the urgency of lived life—a brief inter-
lude of almost indelible intensity—the very condition to which, in

the poems about the "unlived" life, Dunn's daydreams aspire. What makes many of these poems almost heartbreaking to read is that, even in the moments of fully realized experience when life seems almost to have lived up to what it was supposed to be, the speaker is conscious that the condition is temporary, a sort of lie. Underlying the rapture—the suspense of joy—is a note of panic: these moments are too good to be true.

> Those of us who think we know
> the same secrets
> are silent together most of the time,
> for us there is eloquence
> in desire, and for a while
> when in love and exhausted
> it's enough to nod like shy horses
> and come together
> in a quiet ceremony of tongues
>
> it's in disappointment we look for words
> to convince us
> the spaces between stars are nothing
> to worry about,
> it's when those secrets burst
> in that emptiness between our hearts
> and the lumps in our throats.
> And the words we find
> are always insufficient, like love,
> though they are often lovely
> and all we have

In a related poem, sardonically titled "A Romance," Dunn gives us a pastiche of the very kinds of daydreams lovers are apt to share about their future; but, as the list trudges on, it comes to sound

increasingly mechanical, until finally it sounds exhausted, its charm
worn away:

> He called eel grass
> what she called seaweed.
> He insulated their house with it.
> She was interested in
> the transparence of her skin.
> He walled the bathroom
> with barn-siding, he built the couch
> with wood he had chopped.
>
> ....
>
> She baked bread, made jam
> from sugar berries, kept a notebook
> with what she called
> little collections of her breath.
> He said the angle the nail goes in
> is crucial.
> She fed the ducks, called them
> her sentient beings.
>
> ....
>
> He built a bookcase
> for her books.
> They took long walks.

The second section ends with one of Dunn's finest poems, "Coming Home, Garden State Parkway," which serves as a transition from
the "romance" of the second section back to the quotidian world
where life is mostly unlived. Here, as in "Truckstop: Minnesota,"
"home" is in a car moving through a bleak landscape made familiar
and warm only by means of the daydreams piped over the radio and
the daydreams that form in one's head:

Tonight the toll booth men are
congratulating the weather,
wishing me well. I'm all thank you's
and confusion, I don't know what

kind of conspiracy this is.
Then at Howard Johnson's
the pretty cashier apologizes
for the price of coffee. She wants me

to drive carefully, to think of her
on the dark, straight road.
Does she say these things to everyone?
I've done nothing different

and in the mirror
there's the same old face
not even lovers have called handsome,
the same mouth that belies

absolute conviction.
I'm alone, and maybe
there's an underworld of those alone
and maybe tonight I've entered it—

the instant, safe intimacy
guaranteed to move on.
On the car radio
comes a noisy current song

and then an old melodic lie
about love. . . .
. . . .
I'm going 70, the winter outside

is without snow, it's hard anymore
to be sure about anything.
Next toll station, I feel for a quarter—
the exact change

but I swerve
(as I knew I would)
to the woman holding out her hand.
She neither smiles nor speaks,

I try to believe
she's shy.
I'd like to put my hand in her hand,
to keep alive

this strange human streak I'm on.
But there's only money between us,
silver and flesh
meeting in a familiar goodbye.

The marvel is that Dunn is able so flatly to declare our condition without a crack in his voice, without a note of bitterness, without blaming anybody—to write what may be called a "realist lyric" that can feelingly sing about the vast stretches of living in which so little happens, in which we do not feel enough.

In his ability to make disarmingly honest admissions without disgusting or embarrassing us, to bring into the open some of the squalid aspects of the inner life, Dunn might be regarded as a sort of Woody Allen of contemporary American poetry. Like Allen, he manages through an innate gentleness to speak with a certain dignity about the meanest banalities. But the overall tone of Dunn's poetry is not comic or joking. It is, like most of the best lyric poetry, grave. Whereas comedy and wit tend to reduce the spectrum of human emotions to one emotion—laughter—Dunn's lyrics are overflowing with a range of complex emotions, even though they sing about subjects that often seem fit only for satire. Until Dunn's poems, unlived life had never received this kind of serious non-satirical treatment by an American poet. Although poets such as Edgar Lee Masters and, more especially, Edwin Arlington Robinson, might have been able to handle such a theme, daydream was not nearly so great a part of American civilization then as it is now. It was hardly the major industry it is today. The technology had not been invented. When Miniver Cheevy laments that he was not born a "Medici," his fantasy—his sense of missed opportunity—is literary, like the daydreams of Prufrock. It would have been harder for Robinson to write a nonsatirical poem in which Cheevy wished he had been born Joe Namath.

The only recent poet other than Dunn to treat unlived life in a realist manner, without condescension, was Frank O'Hara; and his poems have nowhere near the emotional depth of Dunn's. Instead, they are apt to sound manic or self-consciously gabby, as, for example, his famous "Poem":

> Lana Turner has collapsed!
> I was trotting along and suddenly
> it started raining and snowing
> and you said it was hailing
> but hailing hits you on the head
> hard so it was really snowing and
> raining and I was in such a hurry
> to meet you but the traffic
> was acting exactly like the sky
> and suddenly I see a headline
> LANA TURNER HAS COLLAPSED!
> There is no snow in Hollywood
> there is no rain in California

> I have been to lots of parties
> and acted perfectly disgraceful
> but I never actually collapsed
> oh Lana Turner we love you get up

This is a brilliant poem—a super-realism that catches exactly the hype and tempo of life in Manhattan—in a landscape so artificial that vicarious experience forms the very weather, the rest of the world being a kind of dream piped in by cables and transmitters. But, compared with Dunn's characterless suburban environment, as in his poem "Here and There," where "when the newspaper arrives/ with the world,/ people make kindling of it/ and sit together while it burns," O'Hara's world is abnormal, a special one. The importance of Dunn's poetry is that it covers the other ninety-five percent of the American experience—a neglected terrain seemingly inaccessible to beautiful poetry—and renders so accurately the feeling of being lost at home in the middle of the country.

Notes

1. Christopher Lasch, *The Culture of Narcissism* (New York: W. W. Norton, 1978), pp. 96–97.

2. Ibid., p. 20.

3. The activity of reading I would place in neither category. It requires too much participation, too much initiative, too much mental exercise to be identified as a form of the unlived life; but it is too passive an activity to be identified with the lived life. Even Emerson believed that sailing a boat is a better way to learn to sail than reading about sailing.

4. Louis Simpson, "Rolling Up," in *American Poets in 1976*, ed. William Heyen (Indianapolis: Bobbs-Merrill, 1976), p. 333.

5. Larry Levis, "Some Notes on the Gazer Within," *Field* 19 (Fall 1978): 32.

6. Ibid., p. 37.

Six

SYNTAX AND THE POETRY
OF JOHN ASHBERRY

JOHN ASHBERY IS THE FIRST AMERICAN
poet to carry out successfully the possibilities of analogy between
poetry and abstract-expressionist painting. He has succeeded so well
for two reasons: (1) he is the first poet to identify the correct corre-
spondences between painting and writing; (2) he is the first poet to
explore that analogy who has possessed the skill to produce a first-
rate "abstract-expressionist poetry," a poetry as evocative and sturdy
as the paintings of Willem de Kooning.

It is perhaps de Kooning's early stint as an illustrator that makes
his later, nonrepresentational paintings allude so strongly to familiar
forms and landscapes, to shapes that never quite materialize. Similarly, it is perhaps Ashbery's work as an editor and his ability to
write good prose that lend the paragraphs of his verse their architec-
tonic quality, their relentless sense of being "about" something specific, of moving toward some point that, like the end of a rainbow,
always just eludes us. We derive this sense from an Ashbery poem
mainly because the syntax of his sentences is so reasonable sounding,
so adeptly connected over such long intervals. It is the syntax of the
best expository prose style. Language, fit into such syntax, almost

"Syntax and the Poetry of John Ashbery" originally appeared in *American Poetry Review* 8 (July–August 1979): 37–40, and is reproduced here, with minor changes, by permission.

has to mean something definite. Consider, for example, a passage from his poem "These Lacustrine Cities":

> These lacustrine cities grew out of loathing
> Into something forgetful, although angry with history.
> They are the product of an idea: that man is horrible,
>   for instance,
> Though this is only one example.
>
> They emerged until a tower
> Controlled the sky, and with artifice dipped back
> Into the past for swans and tapering branches,
> Burning, until all that hate was transformed into useless
>   love.

The syntax of this resonant passage stands out more sharply if we read it undistracted by the frame of verse:

> These lacustrine cities grew out of loathing into something forgetful, although angry with history. They are the product of an idea: that man is horrible, for instance, though this is only one example. They emerged until a tower controlled the sky, and with artifice dipped back into the past for swans and tapering branches, burning, until all that hate was transformed into useless love.

It is Ashbery's genius not only to be able to execute syntax with this heft but also to perceive that syntax in writing is the equivalent of composition in painting: it has an intrinsic beauty and authority almost wholly independent of any specific context. Thus, in Ashbery's poetry, the isolation of verse on the page is analogous to the framing of a painting; and each sentence—not each word—each *sentence* is analogous to a brushstroke (or to any discrete gesture) recorded in paint on a canvas.

The basis—the necessary but not sufficient condition—for the credibility of Ashbery's best poems is simply the syntax of his "prose." For it is a curious fact, one that anybody who has ever prescribed "imitation" to students has observed, that beautiful syntax has a habit of dignifying almost any text one substitutes into it. Consider, for example, the following passage from D. H. Lawrence's *Phoenix: The Posthumous Papers*:

> We have our very individuality in relationship. Let us swallow this important and prickly fact. Apart from our connections with other people, we are barely individuals, we amount, all of us, to next to nothing. It is in the living touch between us and other people, other lives, other phenomena that we move and have our being. Strip us of our human contacts and of our contact with the living earth and sun, and we are almost bladders of emptiness. Our individuality means nothing. A skylark that was alone on an island would be songless and meaningless, his individuality gone, running about like a mouse in the grass. But if there were one female with him, it would lift him singing into the air, and restore him his real individuality.
>
> And so with men and women. It is in relationship to one another that they have their true individuality and their distinct being: in contact, not out of contact. This is sex, if you like. But it is no more sex than sunshine on the grass is sex. It is a living contact, give and take: the great and subtle relationship of men and women, man and woman. In this and through this we become real individuals, without it, without the real contact, we remain more or less nonentities.

This passage is typical of Lawrence's style: it is oratorical, full of parallelism and repetition; it has a spellbinding rhythm. A dialectic of contraries is not only the content of the passage but also its form, a gesturing back and forth between dramatic alternatives: "in this . . . without it." The style is perhaps a bit portentous. But even a critic of Lawrence ought to admit that the structure of the passage is handsome. Moreover, its handsomeness is far from dependent on a specific text. In the imitation below, I have substituted the counters "friendship" and "respect" for "individuality" and "relationships":

> Ideal friendship is founded on mutual respect. Let us consider this simple elemental law. Without mutual respect, a social bond is barely sustainable, the social bond adds up to almost nothing. It is from the discreet deference of person to person, human to human that compansionship draws its energy.

Deprive us of our respect for one another and of our awe for the otherness of man and beast, and we are virtually husks of indifference. Our relationships are shriveled. A proud man alone among fools will feel useless and nettled, his potentiality lost, chatting inanely like a magpie in a tree. But if there were one intelligent person with him, it would set his thoughts moving into words, and restore him his rightful dignity.

And so with husband and wife. It is through respect for one another that they build their slow bond and their lasting companionship: from deference, not aggression. This is defensiveness, if you like. But it is no more defensiveness than proper manners at the table is defensiveness. It is an active attentiveness, day and night: the pervasive and intricate contract between husband and wife, human and human. In this and through this we nourish our friendships, without it, without any genuine mutual respect, we remain unfulfilled.

It is obvious from the imitation above that the structure of the Lawrence passage most comfortably accommodates a limited type of subject matter. The thrust of the entire passage is aimed by its first topic sentence, whose main gist is *A* (something desirable or natural) depends on *B* (something seemingly contradictory or, if not contradictory, at least not obvious and perhaps even undesirable). Nevertheless, within that format, a wide vocabulary will work. One can severely strain the format and still emerge with a handsome syntax, as in the following imitation:

Our happiness depends on financial well-being. Let us accept this rather unpleasant truth. Without adequate income, most of us are barely satisfied, we feel, most of us, on the verge of deep despair. It is in the spending of money on extravagant things, on good meals, cars, and clothes that we take our greatest joy. Strip us of our wallets and of our charge cards, and we are mere shadows of our former selves. Our lives are meaningless. An executive without money in Las Vegas would be sad and absurd, his happiness gone, running about like a bird without wings. But if he had one five-hundred-dollar bill, his spirits would soar and return him to true happiness.

This is even true of children. It is in the possession of toys that they find their true happiness and their keenest pleasure: in ownership, not poverty. This is greed, if you like. But it is no more greed than a cat's desire for milk is greed. It is ownership, having and holding: the natural and all-pervasive instinct of adults and children alike. With it, we are happy, without it, without money or material possessions, we remain sad.

Needless to say, this passage lacks some of the dignity of the original. It is, if anything, mock-heroic. What heroism is left, however, springs from what elements of Lawrence's syntax have been preserved.

But what happens if we substitute into Lawrence's format material that lacks any rigorous, logical development, an "argument" whose terms can be connected only figuratively and that are strung together discursively? As the example below should demonstrate, the result will still seem to insist on its own sense, even if we are unable to pin down just what that sense is:

> We become actual through a species of weather. Let us recite again the facts. Divorced from the sky in any landscape, we are scarcely awake, we amount, all of us, to sleepwalkers. It is in the wet touch of our hands to each cloud and gust and season that we shiver and find our perception. Erase the cumulus and blur the high mackerel sky of early evening, and we are but fading frequencies of information. Our being is lessened. Descartes alone in such a desert would be without coordinates, his conceptions fading, thoughtless as sand in the wintery moonlight. But if there were gaudier weathers, his mathematics would spring back with the morning, serve as a workable song.
>
> And so with autumn and slow rains. It is in the lick of wet leaves that our axes are drawn and reflect their distinct effects: in metamorphosis, not in calm. This is storm, if you like. But it is no more storm than the precipitation of light is storm. It is wet contact, ubiquitous, quick: the steady and ultimate procession of colder fronts, changes of wind. In this and through this we become actual, shorn of it, shorn of contact, we grow less and less.

Even clothed with this discursive imagery, the passage retains a sense of meaningfulness. Indeed, whatever force this version has depends almost entirely on the sentence syntax, which, as I have tried to demonstrate, bears a limited relation to the content of the passage.

Let us now consider an example of Ashbery's poetry. The poem below is one I have selected more or less at random. My only consideration was line length. Ashbery's longer-lined poems are, in my opinion, his better poems. Like those poems of Yeats where extended periodic sentences are jammed into a narrow, rhyming measure that works in syncopated counterpoint to the unfolding syntax, Ashberry's best poems are built from the kinds of sentences more apt to be found in great prose than in great poetry:

EVENING IN THE COUNTRY

I am still completely happy.
My resolve to win further I have
Thrown out, and am charged by the thrill
Of the sun coming up. Birds and trees, houses,
These are but the stations for the new sign of being
In me that is to close late, long
After the sun has set and darkness come
To the surrounding fields and hills.
But if breath could kill, then there would not be
Such an easy time of it, with men locked back there
In the smokestacks and corruption of the city.
Now as my questioning but admiring gaze expands
To magnificent outposts, I am not so much at home
With these memorabilia of vision as on a tour
Of my remotest properties, and the eidolon
Sinks into the effective "being" of each thing,
Stump or shrub, and they carry me inside
On motionless explorations of how dense a thing can be,
How light, and these are finished before they have begun
Leaving me refreshed and somehow younger.
Night has deployed rather awesome forces
Against this state of affairs: ten thousand helmeted
                              footsoldiers,
A Spanish armada stretching to the horizon, all
Absolutely motionless until the hour to strike
But I think there is not too much to be said or be done

And that these things eventually take care of themselves
With rest and fresh air and the outdoors, and a good view
        of things.
So we might pass over this to the real
Subject of our concern, and that is
Have you begun to be in the context you feel
Now that the danger has been removed?
Light falls on your shoulders, as is its way,
And the process of purification continues happily,
Unimpeded, but has the motion started
That is to quiver your head, send anxious beams
Into the dusty corners of the rooms
Eventually shoot out over the landscape
In stars and bursts? For other than this we know nothing
And space is a coffin, and the sky will put out the light.
I see you eager in your wishing it the way
We may join it, if it passes close enough:
This sets the seal of distinction on the success or failure
        of your attempt.
There is growing in that knowledge
We may perhaps remain here, cautious yet free
On the edge, as it rolls its unblinking chariot
Into the vast open, the incredible violence and yielding
Turmoil that is to be our route.

There is much more to this poem than syntax, just as there is much more to a de Kooning painting than composition. The poem is referential; it alludes richly to the world.

The mood of "Evening in the Country" is expansive, pastoral, meditative, philosophical. As its title confirms, there is a rambling, rural amplitude of vision here, a grand, romantic solitude strongly reminiscent of Wordsworth's "Tintern Abbey" or of parts of *The Prelude*. The poem presents to us an experience, a gestalt of color, scale, emotion, tempo that seems wholly familiar, wholly recognizable, with innumerable precedents both in literature and in our own lives; yet, if we examine the poem at all, can we say with any confidence that it is describing a literal "evening in the country"? Could not "the country" figuratively suggest the United States or, indeed, any landscape, real or imaginary? The figurative associations of "evening" are, of course, too numerous and too obvious to mention. In line four we get further encouragement not to refer the language of this poem to any single context: "Birds and trees, houses,/ These are but the stations for the new sign of being/ In me that is to close late, long/ After the sun has set and darkness come/ To the surrounding fields and hills." To put it differently, "These" (words) are "stations" for "a new sign of being," for a sea change of the psyche that may be abstracted from any specific set of circumstances. The poem alludes to the world, but its range of possible reference is unlimited. The referents all lie outside the poem.

This brings us to the basic assumption, the central paradox, on which the abstract-expressionist aesthetic is founded: the assumption that a work of art can present to us a gestalt that is recognizable without reference to a specific context, which can be general yet feel specific. The strategy of Ashbery's mature work relentlessly strives to achieve this degree of "abstraction," of absolution. "Evening in the Country" establishes it by line twelve: "Now as my questioning but admiring gaze expands/ To magnificent outposts, I am not so much at home/ With these memorabilia of vision as on a tour/ Of my remotest properties. . . ." At this point the poem's expansive gestures establish a sweeping scale of vision independent of any "fields" or "houses." The evocative phrase "my remotest properties" has an infinite range of reference. The tempo of the language and the very syntax of the sentences—the long, unfurling sense of settling down that they give—constitute a precise and convincing "objective correlative" to our experience, but—that paradox again—an objective correlative with only one term. Inevitably, Ashbery's diction is abstract; yet, despite its degree of abstraction, the passage is strangely concrete. It is as if, just below the "surface" of the "painting," there were a specific landscape, a single occasion, on the verge of breaking through but never quite able to. It is the implicit and imminent presence of this world, trying to come back through the poem, that gives Ashbery's poetry much of its suspense. De Kooning's paintings have a similar suspense. One feels as if one were observing a familiar landscape in a familiar light, yet the landscape contains no hills, no buildings, no sky, no recognizable objects.

The freedom, the absolution that such a strategy confers may be appreciated if we compare it with the strategy of Wallace Stevens in "Sea Surface Full of Clouds." In each of the five sections of the Stevens poem, a different mood is projected upon a fixed scene consisting of three elements: deck, sea, sky. The poem has the orderliness of a mathematical demonstration. It is like a polynomial function of x that, while it retains its structure, assumes a different "value" for each numerical value substituted for x. The physical world, the "scene" of deck, sea, and sky, comprises the independent variable; each of the five different qualities of "light" that strike the scene is a numerical value of x, transformed by the imagination (f) into $f(x)$. I draw this mathematical analogy because it seems to me that Stevens' intent in this poem is, like Ashbery's, to abstract feeling and to free it as fully as possible from any context, to make feeling absolute. Stevens tries here, as best he can, to minimize context by keeping it invariant, by treating it like a movie screen onto which pure feeling can be projected; but the shipboard scene never completely vanishes, and we are left with five separate romantic vignettes, five scenes of the sea altered by what Wordsworth would call "a certain colouring of imagination." The very presence of "imagery," of a "scene," causes us to refer feeling to elements *in* the poem, to a picture. In an Ashbery poem, on the other hand, "the scene" onto which "feeling" is projected is no longer a set of images that can be located within the verse frame. Instead, as the title of Ashbery's best collection, *Self-Portrait in a Convex Mirror* (1975), would suggest, what corresponds to the scene in the Stevens poem—the designated area upon which the imagination throws its "colouring"—is the very syntax of the poem, which disarms the reader, lending an Ashbery poem the same air of reasonableness that conventional imagery lends the Stevens poem. In an Ashbery poem, the contexts to which the "colouring" can be applied are, like the images in a conventional mirror, *outside* the frame, and, like the images in a convex mirror, they have an unlimited range of reference: every object within a 180-degree angle of vision behind the person facing the mirror appears in the mirror. Indeed, the difference between Ashbery's aesthetic and Stevens' is not so great. Ashbery's aesthetic is simply the next logical step beyond Stevens'.

But the analogy we have been pursuing between Ashbery's epistemology and the epistemology of abstract-experessionist painting may be carried a step further: If the choice of a verse format is equivalent to the imposition of a frame upon a painted area and if Ashbery's interlocking sentence patterns are equivalent to a kind of painterly composition within the frame, then to what do individual sentences correspond? To brushstrokes, to discrete painterly gestures recorded by whatever means—brush, rag, palette knife. To extend the analogy yet another step: The "content" of an Ashbery sentence may then be regarded as similar to the "content" of a brushstroke in a painting.

Beyond the obvious and trivial fact that, in abstrract-expressionist painting a brushstroke is the record of a process, a moment in the history of the painting, do brushstrokes have referential "content?" Yes. As they are intended to, they refer, like the images in a mirror (convex or otherwise), to anything and everything outside the frame. Indeed, the very act of "framing" is a convention fundamental to both literature and painting, a convention that directs our habits of reference, that tells us what to expect when confronting a painting, a novel, a poem. So established is this convention in painting that it is impossible to look at a framed painting without trying to find a "picture," without thinking that the painting, like a paragraph of complete sentences, must be "about" something and that everything within the frame coheres in one "image." As a result, one is continually brought up short by the surface and texture of an abstract-expressionist painting. The eye involuntarily looks through the picture plane to find a scene, only to be yanked back to the surface, to be reminded that there is, within the frame, no image, no illusion against which to compare the paint, nothing whose verisimilitude need be judged; and yet the impulse to locate an image persists. The entire picture plane buzzes with rumors of the world while furnishing nothing more definite than the motions of paint, brushstrokes that, although they are clearly about the world, are unimpeachable representatives of it because they do not have to "look like" any one thing, because they look like anything: they are absolved from the meanness of narrow reference.

The "content" of Ashbery's best sentences has a similar unimpeachability. The sentences make assertions that, like the assertions of brushstrokes, *have* to be true, assertions that, by referring to anything and everything at once, approach the perfect truth of tautology: "But I think there is not too much to be said or be done/ And that these things eventually take care of themselves/. . . ./ There is growing in that knowledge/ We may perhaps remain here, cautious yet free/ On the edge. . . ." In order to assess this kind of proposition, we must first recognize that it is endemic to much contemporary poetry. Consider, for example, the grim wit of William Stafford's "Ozymandias's Brother." The "brother" of "Ozymandias" is, in this poem, a metaphor for any ordinary person. Most of the poem is devoted to the problem of deciphering the words on his "tomb," even though "(he hardly has a tomb)." At one point the speaker of the poem remarks: "He was here for a while, then gone. That's/ about the right degree of assertion, holding forth/ what there is, no despair." The poem ends: "I'd put them on the tomb the same./. . . Here's what I think it says:/ 'Anyway, it was the world.'" The entire poem is, then, about the question of what we can say with any confidence about our condition and to what "degree of assertion" we can say it. The poem's final sentence has the perfect unimpeachability of an Ashbery sentence. If it appears different, it is only because Stafford's entire poem reveals the process by which this proposition has been derived whereas an Ashbery poem begins a step later: in Ashbery the derivation of such an epistemology is taken for granted, and an entire poem consists of this kind of proposition.

One of the best examples of this kind of unimpeachable proposition that recurs so regularly in contemporary poetry is the last sentence of Alan Dugan's "Poem":

> What's the balm
> for a dying life,
> dope, drink, or Christ,
> is there one?
>
> I puke and choke
> with it and find
> no peace of mind
> in flesh, and no hope.
>
> It flows away
> in mucous juice.
> Nothing I can do
> can make it stay,
>
> so I give out
> and water the garden: it

is all shit
for the flowers anyhow.

In the second stanza, "it" seems to refer to "a dying life." In the third stanza, "it" refers also to "flesh" and "hope." In the last stanza, "I give out" suggests first of all "I die" and "water the garden" (the "garden" is here the world) with my own "mucous juice." "I give out" suggests also: my anger at the absence of a "balm" "gives out" and I decide to behave constructively, to tend "the garden" (which may be a literal one but which may also be the world at large, where things flower and perish), to act as if I had a future, even though I know I don't. By the time we reach the last sentence, the accumulated context in which "it" occurs, combined with the abstraction of "the flowers" and the suggestiveness of "anyhow" (used here as Stafford uses "anyway"), gives the statement an endless range of reference. The unimpeachability of this proposition—everything is shit for flowers anyhow—is cinched by the echo of that most conventional paradox: that "shit" is for "flowers" suggests, among other things, that "death" breeds "life." But the line is typical of Dugan and of much post-modernist poetry in that it does not advance this paradox as a "solution" or as some hard-earned reconciliation. Dugan advances it as only a cold fact, the only proposition that can be derived from examination of the evidence, and the possibility of renewal in "the flowers" is totally neutralized by the colloquial connotations of "it is all shit."

In Dugan's poetry, irony is the pre-eminent condition from which we speak. Dugan's poems begin in irony and work through it to a posture beyond it. Since every proposition in Dugan's poem is ironical—since irony is the norm of discourse—all the ironies tend to cancel each other out, and the poem is able, in the end, to combine all possible tones—rage, grief, frustration, sarcasm, wonder, resignation, cynicism, joy, and so on—into one bald, bleak, toneless, absolute assertion, in much the same way that all the colors of the spectrum combine to produce white. Similarly, the tone—the color—is "white" when, at the end of his ominously offhanded poem "In Memory of the Utah Stars," William Matthews says:

> You never lose your touch
> or forget how taxed bodies
> go at the same pace they owe,
> how brutally well the universe
> works to be beautiful,
> how we metabolize loss
> as fast as we have to.

Where Matthews's and Dugan's and Stafford's poems end marks the epistemological ground—the realm of discourse with its endless, noncommittal "white" propositions—on which Ashbery's poetry begins, a poetry whose formal characteristics are, like those of abstract-expressionist painting, not an arbitrary experiment but the result of Ashbery's anxiety over what Stafford calls, in "Ozymandias's Brother," "the right degree of assertion." A fairly convincing case could be made that the development of photography forced painting to become figurative, that the emergence of abstract expressionism constituted an implicit recognition by painters that, in the business of producing journalistically accurate pictures, they could no longer compete with photographers. An abstract-expressionist poetry must derive from a similar sense, among its practitioners, of the dead-endedness and epistemological limitation of "representational" propositions, of propositions that confidently assert the speaker's stance, that risk an opinion. It is this metaphysical hedging—a kind of despair, if you will, or at least a refusal to risk making a fool of oneself by earnestly trying to mean something—that lies behind the cool, noncommittal lyricism of so much plain-style verse. But in Ashbery's poetry we see that there is a degree of epistemological despair beyond which the formal assumptions of "representational" poetry can no longer apply.

Seven

"INSTANT WORDSWORTH"

Is the conservatism that we have seen in every aspect of American life in the late 1970s visible also in our poetry? Are most American poets cranking out a tasteful but complacent minor poetry? Such a sobering prognosis is strongly implicit in some remarks made by Marjorie Perloff at the 1978 proceedings of the Modern Language Association, where, zeroing in on a poem by Richard Hugo as typical of the breed, she characterized "the overwhelming majority of the poems appearing in literary magazines" as "conservative, instant Wordsworth."

When I heard this charge, my immediate impulse was to wonder with a sinking heart whether she was right; for, as Perloff suggests, much of our poetry today might well, at first glance, have been written using Wordsworth's "Preface to the *Lyrical Ballads*" as a manual. In Daniel Halpern's *American Poetry Anthology* (1975), for example, the vast majority of poems are in the first-person singular, featuring the poet as protagonist, as, in the phrase of Wordsworth, "a man speaking to men." The vast majority of poems conform to the criteria Wordsworth sets forth in the "Preface": they "choose incidents and situations from common life," "relate or describe them" in open-form verse "in a selection of language really used by men," and "throw over them a certain colouring of imagination, whereby ordinary things" are "presented to the mind in an unusual aspect." In most of these poems "the feeling therein developed gives importance to the action and situation, and not the action and situation to the feeling," and they attempt to imitate a "spontaneous overflow of powerful feelings."

The Hugo poem that Perloff picked on is the following piece from Hugo's collection *31 Letters and 13 Dreams* (1977):

IN YOUR YOUNG DREAM

You are traveling to play basketball. Your team's
a good one, boys you knew when you were young.
A game's in Wyoming, a small town, a gym
in a grammar school. You go in to practice.
No nets on the hoops. You say to the coach,
a small man, mean face, "We need nets on the rims."
He sneers as if you want luxury. You explain
how this way you can't see the shots go in.
You and another player, vaguely seen, go out
to buy nets. A neon sign on a local tavern
gives directions to the next town, a town
a woman you loved lives in. You go to your room
to phone her, to tell her you're here just
one town away to play ball. She's already
waiting in your room surrounded by children.
She says, "I'll come watch you play ball."
Though young in the dream you know you are old.
You are troubled. You know you need nets on the rims.

Perloff's observations about the poem were that (1) it has "nothing to do with the present," that (2) despite its date of publication, it is "pre-modernist," and that (3) although it is framed as a dream, it is "non-dreamlike" because it is a "rationalized dream." Perloff presented each of these observations as though it were an invidious distinction.

In a gesture designed to show that she was indeed trying to represent fairly the full range of contemporary American poetry, Perloff then compared the Hugo piece to one of John Berryman's Dream Songs:

OP. POSTH. NO. 2

In a blue series towards his sleepy eyes
they slid like wonder, women tall & small,
of every shape & size,
in many languages to lisp 'We do'
to Henry almost waking. What is the night at all,
his closed eyes beckon you.

In the Marriage of the Dead, a new routine,
he gasped his crowded vows past lids shut tight
and a-many rings fumbled on.
His coffin like Grand Central to the brim
filled up & emptied with the lapse of light.
Which one will waken him?

O she must startle like a fallen gown,
content with speech like an old sacrament
in deaf ears lying down,
blazing through darkness till he feels the cold
& blindness of his hopeless tenement
while his black arms unfold.

Perloff characterized this poem as "late-modernist" with "a slight swerve inward." Although "Freudian," it is, Perloff contended, "not dreamlike either," but "still coherent."

To present a contrast to the Berryman and the Hugo poems,

Perloff then adduced a passage from Samuel Beckett's *How It Is* (1964) as an example of "early post-modernist form" and, finally, dealt with the following poem by John Ashbery:

ON THE TOWPATH

At the sign "Fred Muffin's Antiques" they turned off the
road into a narrow lane lined with shabby houses.

If the thirst would subside just for awhile
It would be a little bit, enough.
This has happened.
The insipid chiming of the seconds
Has given way to an arc of silence
So old it had never ceased to exist
On the roofs of buildings, in the sky.

The ground is tentative.
The pygmies and jacaranda that were here yesterday
Are back today, only less so.
It is a barrier of fact
Shielding the sky from the earth.

On the earth a many-colored tower of longing rises.
There are many ads (to help pay for all this).
Something interesting is happening on every landing.
Ladies of the Second Empire gotten up as characters from Perrault:
Red Riding Hood, Cinderella, the Sleeping Beauty,
Are silhouetted against the stained-glass windows,
A white figure runs to the edge of some rampart
In a hurry only to observe the distance,
And having done so, drops back into the mass
of clock-faces, spires, stalactite machiolations.
It was the walking sideways, visible from far away,

That told what it was to be known
And kept, as a secret is known and kept.

The sun fades like the spreading
Of a peacock's tail, as though twilight
Might be read as a warning to those desperate
For easy solutions. This scalp of night
Doesn't continue or break off the vacuous chatter
That went on, off and on, all day:

....

Perloff's account of this poem was generally complimentary. She pointed out that the piece exhibits "erasure," "discontinuity," "randomness," "incoherence" and that the "irony" in Ashbery's poetry is that it will "present contradictions as parallels which needn't be reconciled." The resulting poems are, she said, unlike the "rationalized dreams" of Hugo or of Berryman, "irreducible," their very irreducibility being "in the service of a redemptive enchantment."

If we review the Perloff presentation, the thrust of it seems, at first glance, to amount to a fairly plausible position. She seems to be asserting that, from the pre-moderism (anachronistically represented by Hugo) through the modernism epitomized (for her) by the Berryman poem to the post-modernism (its inevitability suggested by the Beckett poem, its full potential exemplified in the Ashbery poem), poetic form has progressively accommodated the irrational, the discontinuous, the irreconcilable. There are, of course, some implicit value judgments in this diagnosis. In her criticism of the two non-post-modernist poems for their "coherence" and in her identification of irreducibility with "enchantment," she would seem to be arguing not only that the content of a good poem is necessarily irreducible but also that lack of coherence is, if not the exact equivalent of irreducibility, then a desirable form of it. In her allegation that Hugo is "conservative," she would seem to value innovation for its own sake.

More surprising, perhaps, than these value judgments, which are hardly original, is Perloff's use of the term "modernism." "Modernism" has, to me at least, come to denote a poetic based roughly on the position Eliot outlined in "Tradition and the Individual Talent": a poetic that involves "extinction of the personality" so that in most of the famous modernist poems the poet's personality and presence is so peripheral as to be scarcely noticeable, the poems being composed, like Pound's *Cantos* or Eliot's *Waste Land*, of shored-together fragments of The Tradition. "Late-Modernism" customarily refers to the kind of poetry that dominates the first edition of *New Poets of England and America* (1957), a learned, highly wrought poetry epitomized perhaps by the work of Richard Wilbur, of the early Berryman, of the Robert Lowell who antedates *Life Studies* (1959). Late-modernism, then, consists of a genteel and mildly academic refinement of the modernist canon, preserving the impersonality and erudition of modernism while domesticating its form into a graceful metric. When Perloff describes the Berryman poem as evincing "a slight swerve inward," it seems to me that she is drastically understating the poem's inwardness. Although the Berryman piece, like all poetry after modernism, assimilates the lessons of modernism and exhibits extensive evidence of modernist technique—particularly in the demand it makes upon the reader to supply missing connections, to piece together the poem as if from fragments—it is really closer to the confessional mode than to the modernist, or even the late-modernist, mode. In applying the term "late-modernist" to Berryman, Perloff would seem to be excluding from her concept of "modernist" any consideration of the degree to which the poet places himself in his poem. According to her line of reasoning, a poem would be categorized pre-modernist, modernist, or post-modernist on the basis of a much narrower concept of form.

She would categorize poems only according to their degrees of "ambiguity" and "discontinuity." In this view, the more discontinuity a poem displays, the more advanced it is in the development of American poetry. Such a narrow concept of poetic form, measuring only the breadth of a poem's synapses, the thickness of its ironies, the number of laminations in its ambiguities, makes it possible to discover, in the diversity of our poetry, a neat but reductive appearance of order, a steady line of development from pre-modernism through the complexities of modernism to the discontinuities of post-modernism, in which the prefix *post-* can not only refer to a poem's formal elements; *post-* can also carry some of the historical associations it always seemed to demand. It can mean "after" modernism.

Perloff's position, as I have outlined it above, would be compelling if it were not undermined by a single, overwhelming contradiction: although her concept of "form" purports to be exclusively structural rather than rhetorical and does not take into consideration the position or stance the poet assumes in the poem, we sense that, when she relegates Hugo to the status of a pre-modernist, she does so precisely *because* of the degree to which the poem *is* personal and confessional—the rhetoric of "a man speaking to men"—rather than because it is "rationalized." "Pre-modernist," according to Perloff's approach, refers to any poem in which the author frankly declares his or her presence and speaks in an ostensibly autobiographical manner. This is why, in her remarks on the Hugo poem, Perloff fails to notice any modernist (or even post-modernist) tendencies, when, in fact, they are quite pronounced. This is why, as an example of the poetry of the 1960s, Perloff has chosen a Berryman poem rather than, say, a Lowell poem—because Berryman's style exhibits so many modernist tendencies, including the elaborate Henry Pussycat mask. And this is why, from Hugo's work, Perloff has chosen an inferior and rather uncharacteristic poem.

Hugo's best work—although it is, in both its cadences and its content, the most Wordsworthian poetry being written today and although it is certainly more explicitly personal than, say, *The Waste Land* or "Love Calls Us to the Things of This World"—exhibits a profound and sophisticated consciousness of modernist techniques and conventions. In fact, "In Your Young Dream" exhibits not only modernist features but also some elements of post-modernism (as a formal mode rather than as a historical period) that Perloff fails to notice. Far more fundamental both to the post-modernist mode and to all contemporary poetry than such features as "discontinuity," "erasure," and whatnot is the tendency of poets to borrow the form of a poem from a nonliterary source instead of relying on standard literary conventions as a basis for form. Thus the Hugo poem pretends to be, not a poem, but, as its very title indicates, the thumbnail sketch of a dream.

Indeed, the degree to which contemporary poets increasingly seem to feel the need to borrow from a variety of nonliterary conventions is underlined by the title of Hugo's book: *31 Letters and 13 Dreams*. "In Your Young Dream" parodies a nonverse convention just as Ashbery's "On the Towpath" begins by parodying the mode of prose fiction, slips into a parody of *The Waste Land* for a moment, and so on, all the while deriving its fundamental aesthetic from abstract-expressionist painting. What is significant about the Hugo poem is not that it presents a *rationalized* dream but that it presents its data—rationalized or not—in the form of a *dream*. Although some of the dreams and letters in the collection seem to be rough reworkings of actual letters and dreams, some of them do not—for example, the last poem in the book:

ON YOUR GOOD DREAM

From this hill they are clear, the people
in pairs emerging from churches, arm

in soft arm. And limb on green limb
the shade oaks lining the streets form
rainproof arches. All day festive tunes
explain your problems are over. You picnic
alone on clean lawn with your legend.
Girls won't make fun of you here.

Storms are spotted far off enough
to plan going home and home has fire.

It's been here forever. Two leisurely grocers
who never compete. At least ten elms
between houses and rapid grass refilling
the wild field for horses. The same mayor
year after year—no one votes anymore—
stocks bass in the ponds and monster trout
in the brook. Anger is outlawed.
The unpleasant get out. Two old policemen
stop children picking too many flowers
in May and give strangers directions.

....

Obviously the only way to determine whether or not this poem describes an actual dream would be to ask the author; but this poem
is conspicuously less dreamlike than "In Your Young Dream." Indeed, it does not have the feel of a dream at all. Although its form
is the same as that of the other "dreams" in the collection, it lacks
the troubled narrative quality, the element of sequence, common to
the other dreams; it lacks the Freudian typology of a dream. Instead
of letting the energy and the associations latent in its purported
dream imagery speak for themselves, the speaker reports a great deal
of information that is not directly presented in the imagery—for
example, the highly abstract propositions, "Anger is outlawed" and
"The unpleasant get out." Placed as it is at the end of the volume,

this poem imitates the rhetoric of the earlier dream poems, but appears to be a comment on the other dreams. It portrays an ideal world that is too good to be true; but, in the context of the other dreams, it is also portraying a dream that is too good to be a dream. It is, in a sense, one's dream of what a good dream should be: "your good dream" about a dream. To the extent that the poem employs wordplay and whimsey, it is a better poem than the other dream poems, which attempt to transpose dream imagery directly to the cold page. But, stranded there in the daylight, shorn of the energy, of the deep-sea life glow they possess when actually experienced in sleep, these dream images speak rather drily because they must speak for themselves. In "In Your Good Dream," tonality and energy are added through art, and we can glimpse some of the gruff humor, the sardonic quality that, in Hugo's best poems, lends his voice its engagingly human, down-to-earth ring even in the midst of complexity.

Clearly allied with the element of parody in the post-modernist mode is its hypothetical quality, its way of reminding the reader that the text before him is, above all, fictional. Hugo's deployment of the fashionable blurred-you as the governing pronoun in the dream poems has the effect of lending them this hypothetical quality that, in "In Your Young Dream," is augmented by the way in which its title leads into the body of the poem. As a result, though the poem could be construed as autobiography—as the literal transcription of a dream—it lacks the autobiographical feel of, say, Wordsworth's *Prelude*. It resembles a hypothetical and somewhat whimsical fiction rather than testimony.

Perloff's complaint that the Hugo poem is a "rationalized" dream inadvertently underlines the poem's non-Wordsworthian character because it suggests that she reads the poem as one would read a modernist poem—as a kind of puzzle in which the reader is expected to supply the missing links, to supply an interpretation. This *is* the correct way to read the poem. Taken this way, it becomes a parable about the paradox in which an adult might find himself. The nets that the dreamer needs to determine when he makes a basket are metaphors for any set of criteria by which one can know whether or not he has behaved correctly or performed a task right. If his parents, his guardians, are "small" and "mean" and do not supply "nets," a child may have to search for them himself. As he ages, the search may lead him from bar to bar, town to town. It may lead him to seek nets in the responsibilities of family, in the demands of marriage; but, because there were never nets on the rims when he was young, he may not be able to exist comfortably within the rules— the confining entrapment of the nets of wife, family, sustained obligation. Yet, in his instinctive and existential search for order, he may return again and again to the nets he has broken out of, or he may allow himself to be temporarily snared by new ones. Although his adult, rational mind may know full well that there are no absolute nets, the child in a person, buried under layers of habit and good manners, will still instinctively search for the security of the nets: he will "know you need nets on the rims." The penultimate line, "Though young in the dream you know you are old," actually suggests "Though old (an adult) in real life, you are young in your dream life." The fact that the dream, whether consciously contrived, half-remembered and improved upon, or simply transcribed, can be "rationalized" or not has nothing to do with the poem's capacity to serve as "redemptive enchantment." The vision the poem presents has a kind of seedy numinosity that no amount of "rationalization" could dispel. Any rationalization of the piece—for example, the explication above—is best regarded as an interesting though nonessential bonus to the poem, a footnote testifying to its ability to evoke possibility.

Perloff's choice of "In Your Young Dream" to illustrate "instant

Wordsworth" is all the more peculiar because the poem is so un-characteristic of Hugo's work. True, the poem does, in a variety of superficial ways, conform to the criteria that Wordsworth asserts, in his "Preface," he intended to follow. It features the poet as protago-nist, as "a man speaking to men," and the poem does "choose inci-dents and situations from common life" and "relate or describe them . . . in a selection of language really used by men." Moreover, the very content of the poem—dream work—is such that the "ordinary things" of the poet's past are, in his dream, "presented to the mind in an unusual aspect." As we have seen, however, these criteria do not guarantee that the vision of a poem will be as benign as Wordsworth's was. They do not guarantee that the analogue to a poem will be personal testimony, as in Wordsworth's *Prelude* or in his "conversation" poems. This is because the sum and substance of the program set forth by the "Preface" involves primarily considera-tions of rhetoric and only secondarily considerations of form. As a reaction against the neo-classicism and artificiality of the prevailing poetry, the "Preface" merely signals a swing toward a personalized rhetoric, a swing comparable to the swerve, in the 1960s, away from the tired, impersonal, and rather mechanical death rattles of modernism toward a more personal mode of verse. The notion at the heart of the "Preface" has little to do with Romantic Imagination. It is simply the notion that the poet is "a man speaking to men," that it is permissible for a poet to bring his personality, his indi-vidual voice, back into a poem and to place it in a prominent posi-tion. The rest of the "Preface" sets forth the almost self-evident rhetorical principles that follow from this assumption, all of which hinge on the issue of sincerity. If the poet is "a man speaking to men," then the force of his utterance is going to be determined, in large part, by his ethos, which will, necessarily, be measured by his sincerity as much as by his craftmanship. The "feeling" developed in a poem will, necessarily, be regarded as something of an end in itself. Considerations of diction, of language are also related to the consideration of sincerity. When Wordsworth says that personifications are "occasionally prompted by passion" and that he has "made use of them as such," but has rejected them "as a mechanical device of style," he is recognizing the importance of sincerity in a personalized poetic rhetoric.

Any rhetorical stance will, of course, affect poetic form, but these formal consequences will be secondary to it. Thus the notion that poetry should "adopt the very language of men," a notion that has profound formal implications, proceeds from an overall rhetorical assumption and is not itself the basis of a poetic. It is because of the way in which the rhetorical disposition of a poem can influence its form that Perloff confuses the two domains, on the one hand relegating Hugo to the category of pre-modernist by confusing a rhetorical stance with a formal one, on the other hand regarding the late Berryman as a modernist by divorcing considerations of "form" from considerations of rhetoric. The fact is that Hugo is certainly the most Wordsworthian poet we have, yet vintage Hugo could, by no stretch of the imagination or of critical categories, be regarded as pre-modernist. None of Hugo's poems could have been written before *The Waste Land* or Pound or the Fugitives.

Hugo's *The Lady in Kicking Horse Reservoir* (1973) is, in certain superficial ways, so Wordsworthian that it makes me wonder whether all "landscape" poetry tends to present a "scene" whose suffocating literalness in the present is set against the irridescent memory of an imagined landscape—a "scene" both spatially and temporally remote, tantalizing "gleams" of which reappear poignantly in the drab landscape of the present as reminders of how fallen the world may seem to be. The "Montana" that forms the main landscape behind Hugo's book is, of course, the site of what was literally, in its frontier days, a golden age before "the hope of gold/ ran out and men began to pimp," where, in the poem "Helena, Where Homes Go Mad,"

> . . . the lines of some diluted rage
> dice the sky for gawkers on the tour.
> Also shacks. Also Catholic spires,
> the Shriner mosque in answer,
> Reeder's Alley selling earthenware.
> Nowhere gold. Nowhere men strung up.
> Another child delivered, peace,
> the roaring bars and what was love
> is cut away year after year
> or played out vulgar like a game
> the bored make up when laws are firm.

As the passage above suggests, Hugo identifies the played-out gold not only with wealth and greed but also with love and violence. As he says later in the poem, "Someday a man/ might walk away alone from violence/ and gold, shrinking every step."

"Gold," veins of it leading into poem after poem, constitutes the most resonant symbol in the book. Like the haunting "visionary gleams" that flash through Wordsworth's "Ode," it becomes implicated with the sunlight in the water of the rivers that, throughout the collection, hold, with their mystic fish, the thin yet still tantalizing hints of promise left. Just as the "visonary gleams" that recur in Wordsworth's poems comprise the evanescent memories of a "Nature" feminine and maternal, so in Hugo's poems the motif of gold, translated into images of "blondes" and "girls," is a figure for the speaker's obsessive yearning for the feminine: "gold promises of what a kiss would be." In "Where Mission Creek Runs Hard for Joy," a poem addressed to "Joy Twetan," the speaker says, "I fight the sudden cold diminished light/ with flashbacks of a blonde"; and a few lines later, in much the same way that Hart Crane enlarges Pocahontas, Hugo invests his blonde with mythic lineaments:

WAS IT YOU

across this table now, all centuries of what
all men find lovely, Mongolian and Serb,
invested in your face still pink from
the winds' slap and that sadistic wheat?
Money's in the creek. Gold stones magnify
to giant coins, and you poise gold alone
on rock above the wealthy water

There are, in these poems, two ways to "fight the cold diminished light," the deadness, the despair of this "flat and friendless north" that is "home because some people/ go to Perma and come back/ from Perma saying Perma/ is no fun" and where "Any morning brings the same, a test of stamina,/ your capacity to live the long day out": one can literally escape by means of travel; or one can, in this wasteland, haunt the streams from whose obscure and faintly gold-implicated deeps one can occasionally tease a minor revelation, a moment of sustenance that, like the tongue of a lover or the thrashing of a fish on a line, makes one come alive as one tastes, for a moment, the uncontrollable mystery.

In *The Lady in Kicking Horse Reservoir*, woman—the missing female principle for which throughout the volume the poet fishes in order to complete himself, to moisten his life against the feeling of sexual and personal barrenness—is identified with the breeding, healing power of water, fused with it much as, in Theodore Roethke's "Words for the Wind," the entire physical world is animated and revivified with the numinosity of his lover. In the following passage, Hugo's woman is literally under water:

Not my hands but green across you now.
Green tons hold you down, and ten bass curve
teasing in your hair. Summer slime

will pile deep on your breast. Four months of ice
will keep you firm. I hope each spring
to find you tangled in those pads
pulled not quite loose by the spillway pour,
stars in dead reflection off your teeth.

In "Upper Voight's, To All the Cutthroat There"—a poem alto-
gether as excellent as the book's title poem—fish, gold, and woman
are beautifully and poignantly intertwined into a song that is at once
sexual, religious, and about poetry. The poem is, as the title suggests, addressed "to" the "cutthroat" Hugo wants to catch, but it is
also, we sense, addressed to the Muses and to all the women who
"curve away when I approach":

You curve in dandelion wine and in
my dream of a receptive east. Windows
in my house are sanctuary and the four
hills east are fast with creeks
you live in. Why curve tornado from
the shade of cress of stone, why curve away
when I approach upwind, a bush toward
your home, that home of words in back
of any rock that pools the water dark?

I sneak fat and weightless on the log
you're under. I taste the chinese red
of thunder on your throat, jet spots
on your side that fade to spotless white
along your gut. What prayer brings you roaring
quick as words, unexpected, cruel
through gold? God is small. The wing
of eastbound liners six miles over us
as rigid as your fin when you don't move.

The poem ends:

> Vine maple, greasewood
> and my past including last night
> work against my search. And still I look,
> certain you'll leave me, a bitter nun
> starved for curve in my poem.

Fish, woman, Muse, God, the self, all words, all poems, suspended in the medium of golden promise and faith, lurk behind the rigid, masculine fixity of the rock that casts its dark shadow on the fertile water. The vision of the fish, of "the chinese red/of thunder on your throat," is ecstatic, of the Holy, and the prayer that brings the "quick as words" vision is probably the netting of a poem—an "unexpected" fusion of vision and language—but a poem that comes only after the embittering patience of a "nun." Hugo's image of himself as a nun suggests the sustained devotion which art of this caliber requires; it suggests the degree to which fishing is, for him, both literally and figuratively a sacramental act; and the word "bitter" suggests the cost of art—the kind of chastity it can exact—and also the ache of uncompleted sexuality that runs like a single low note through the entire book.

In "The Gold Man on the Beckler"—a poem astonishingly reminiscent of the leech-gathering episode in Wordsworth's "Resolution and Independence"—the motifs of gold (both literal and figurative), water, and fish are beautifully intertwined:

> Let him pan. His sluice will rot and flake.
> Here, the gold is river, coiling gold
> around gold stones or bouncing gold down
> flat runs where the riffles split the light.
> With just that shack he built beside the stream
> how could he get so fat? Where's the food from?

Why so cheerful with a flimsy roof,
no money and that crude hair in his ears?
....

If I could live like him, my skin stained gold
from this gold stream, I'd change my name.
I have to find a trout or something bright
but hidden by refraction, heavier than sin.
That's why today, my last day here,
while he is rinsing blankets in the river,
before I go that long east to my gold
I shout my best goodbye across the roar.

Hugo's reaction to the Gold Man is rather different from
Wordsworth's reaction to the Leech-gatherer, however, and it is in
this difference that we can begin to perceive some of the significant
differences between Hugo's poetry and Wordsworth's. "Resolution
and Independence" ends:

I could have laughed myself to scorn to find
In that decrepit Man so firm a mind.
'God,' said I, 'be my help and stay secure;
I'll think of the Leech-gatherer on the lonely moor!'

The figure the Gold Man cuts, on the other hand, is ridiculous, the
figure of a man so obsessed with the prospect of gold that he has
given up everything to continue his quest, taken leave of his common sense. In his steady pursuit of the ideal, the Gold Man is
as cheerful and cracked as Don Quixote. Whereas Wordsworth's
memory of the Leech-gatherer is as reverent as his yearning toward
the fading gleams of childhood and toward union with Nature is
solemn, the admiration Hugo evinces toward the Gold Man is
tinged with amusement, even condescension; for Hugo's taste for
"gold" is rather more complex and double-edged than Wordsworth's.

Whereas in Wordsworth's poems the celestial light of childhood is a visionary source capable of sustaining him as an adult ("the child is the father of the man"), in Hugo's poems, even though the bitter devotion to an elusive gold can lend his invocation to "all the cutthroat" an edge of sorrow, his quest for "promise," "violence," "gold," "blondes," elemental fish, "kiss," and "curve" is, more often than not, an ironic one. When, in the Mission Creek poem, Hugo writes, "In your wine old fields of wheat replay/ gold promises of what a kiss would be. In your face/ a horse still flogs your face," we hear a note of disillusionment. None of the "gold promises," historical or personal, have ever come true. And, as an adult surveying the remains of towns where gold ran out, seeing in the derelict landscape a metaphor for the way in which people plunder their own bodies for transitory dreams, Hugo is fiercely conscious of the vanity of human life, including his own. Despite the note of pure poignancy Hugo occasionally strikes, the irony and the bitterly sardonic tone ("On bad days in the bar/ you drink until you are mayor") that inform the poems are anything but Wordsworthian.

In "Ghosts at Garnet," for example, the "gold" motif is treated in a thoroughly symbolist fashion, the ironies are as studied and as exhausted as in any John Crowe Ransom poem, the quirky leaping by which the poem establishes itself as a single complex metaphor, letting the reader complete the connections, is wholly modernist, and some of the lines, in their cryptic, abstract quality, have the elegant but bogus philosophical grandeur—the same self-cancelling quality—of the best lines of Ashbery. The poem, which describes an abandoned gold-mining town, begins:

> Shacks are brown, big where things were sold,
> wheat or girls, small where miners lived.
> Some fell while we were crawling up the hill.
> ....
>   A man who missed the vein
> two feet was found by golden friends.

Pines are staking claims. Hard rock men
went harder hearing Chinese sticks explode.
The suicide, two feet from girls, believed
east eyes can see through rock. A hawk
was oriental, swinging far too silent
when the mail arrived.

The poem ends:

For weeds all Mays are equal yellow.
Beneath our skin, gold veins
run wild to China. That false front on
the bar that stands is giving. Ghosts are drinking,
reading postcards, claiming stakes in men.

"Gold" is introduced with a literal meaning; then, with "golden
friends," is extended to stand for the living; then, with "two feet
from girls," to stand for the dream of high living; then, with "A
hawk was oriental," to equal only empty promise; then, with "equal
yellow," to stand for life itself; and, finally, with "gold veins," to
refer to our own bodies and their desires, to the bodies of the dead
under our feet, to the unrecoverable gold in the ground, to all desire—all life that inevitably equals death—to vanity. In such a line
as "For weeds all Mays are equal yellow," we see, however, a phe-
nomenon that crops up frequently in our poetry now—a noncommittal epistemology that declines to differentiate between "fiction"
and history. This epistemology is familiar to us in the works of
fabulators such as John Barth and Donald Barthelme, but among
poets it is far more pronounced in Ashbery than in his peers, as, for
example, in the following passage:

The insipid chiming of the seconds
Has given way to an arc of silence
So old it had never ceased to exist
On the roofs of buildings, in the sky.

Both the Ashbery passage and the Hugo line are as irrefutable as tautology; they parody good sense, not in order to ridicule it, but merely to recapitulate it from the vantage point of some aesthetic distance so that each proposition, while it retains its handsome phrasing and a certain high-flown character, has lost its assertiveness. It has become arbitrary, of primarily aesthetic interest. Obviously the Hugo line is far more locked into a context than is the Ashbery passage, which is not strictly bound by any context but only appears to be because, as a complete sentence, it seems to be in a kind of apposition to its antecedent sentence, "This has happened." Nevertheless, it is this epistemological lack of assertiveness in the two passages and their quality of being serious parody that constitute the essence of the post-modernist style, a style far more pervasive than most critics such as Perloff realize.

To see that style at its best, we need not always turn to Ashbery. The last poem in *The Lady in Kicking Horse Reservoir*—a poem that, I think, has the beauty and stature of Stevens' "The Idea of Order at Key West"—exhibits in a seemingly Wordsworthian way, the serious-parodic mode:

DEGREES OF GRAY IN PHILIPSBURG

You might come here Sunday on a whim.
Say your life broke down. The last good kiss
you had was years ago. You walk these streets
laid out by the insane, past hotels
that didn't last, bars that did, the tortured try
of local drivers to accelerate their lives.
Only churches are kept up. The jail
turned 70 this year. The only prisoner
is always in, not knowing what he's done.

The principal supporting business now
is rage. Hatred of the various grays

the mountain sends, hatred of the mill,
The Silver Bill repeal, the best liked girls
who leave each year for Butte. One good
restaurant and bars can't wipe the boredom out.
The 1907 boom, eight going silver mines,
a dance floor built on springs—
all memory resolves itself in gaze,
in panoramic green you know the cattle eat
or two stacks high above the town,
two dead kilns, the huge mill in collapse
for fifty years that won't fall finally down.

Isn't this your life? That ancient kiss
still burning out your eyes? Isn't this defeat
so accurate, the church bell simply seems
a pure announcement: ring and no one comes?
Don't empty houses ring? Are magnesium
and scorn sufficient to support a town,
not just Philipsburg, but towns
of towering blondes, good jazz and booze
the world will never let you have
until the town you came from dies inside?

Say no to yourself. The old man, twenty
when the jail was built, still laughs
although his lips collapse. Someday soon,
he says, I'll go to sleep and not wake up.
You tell him no. You're talking to yourself.
The car that brought you here still runs.
The money you buy lunch with,
no matter where it's mined, is silver
and the girl who serves you food
is slender and her red hair lights the wall.

Here silver replaces gold; but, as in the other poems, the myth of a
literal golden age ("The 1907 boom") is fused with the speaker's

obsessive memory of a personal "golden age" epitomized by an "ancient kiss/ still burning," to suggest in the most ironic voice the vanity of human desire, desire that yet persists in flagrant disregard of the speaker's awareness that what he desires *is* vanity.

Not only is that paradox dramatized in the poem's question-and-answer debate: it is dramatized also, and even more poignantly, in the poem's very music. Of all our poets, Hugo is one of a handful in this country who is willing and able to forge beautiful lines, to create hauntingly lovely sounds, sounds so gorgeous that one may wonder whether they are appropriate to such bleak themes. But it does not take much reflection to see that Hugo's music is more than appropriate to his theme: it fully embodies it. The cadences of "Degrees of Gray in Philipsburg," for example, are the booming, resonant, iambic cadences of a "golden age." Although his dialect, containing words such as "blondes," "booze," and so on, is distinctly American and modern, the sonorous, rolling, almost bombastic pentameter lodged loosely in the seams of the verses, often turning the corner from one line into the next, harks back not just to Wordsworth; at moments, it is positively Miltonic: "but towns/ of towering blondes, good jazz and booze/ . . . until the town you came from dies inside." Yet the net effect is not mock-heroic. It is one of self-mockery. Even as he sees in the landscape of Philipsburg his own future—his own "life broke down"—the speaker of the poem is eying "the girl that serves you food." He is denying the future he knows will come. He is desiring the very "gold" he knows is deadly. And this sardonic paradox is exemplified in his very prosody. He is persisting in a golden-age tongue as anachronistic and cracked as the religion of the Gold Man, even as he corrupts with his diction and his imagery the pure ore he is dreaming, converting the gold coming out of his mouth into tin. This is serious parody—as serious and beautiful a parody as Prokofiev's "Classical Symphony" is of Mozart.

In poetry of this quality, where feeling and idea are so deeply assimilated in music, "form" and "content" become as nearly identical as is possible in lyric poetry, so intertwined that the experience the poem furnishes the reader is, to borrow Perloff's term, "irreducible." It is not, however, "irreducible" in quite the sense that Perloff seems to mean when she praises Ashbery's "On the Towpath" for its "discontinuity." It is a mistake, I think, to praise a poem as "irreducible" simply because the poem displays such "discontinuity" and "erasure" that it cannot be understood. Generally, in a poem, it is feeling, not exposition, that is irreducible to paraphrase. The best poetry, whether by Wordsworth, by Berryman, or by Hugo, may be easy to understand but still be irreducible to explication in the same sense that the content of music cannot adequately be described in words; for music is, perhaps, the one art in which form *is* content: "sad" in music means "in a minor key."

As the term "lyric poetry" suggests, verse aspires to a condition like that of music, though common sense reminds us that, because the medium of verse—language—is referential, a poem can never stop meaning and just "be." In poetry, form can, of course, reinforce and enrich content, and the art of poetry consists mainly of the art of infusing feeling into language so that, without the aid of external devices such as the author's actual voice in performance, language on a silent page can attain the power and immediacy of a singing voice in the ear of the reader. But, because language is inherently referential, the reader is always going to look for meaning and coherence where he finds grammar. To deny the reader coherence in a poem is to forfeit most of the potentiality of the medium of language, and to do so unnecessarily; for, as "Degrees of Gray in Philipsburg" illustrates, a poem can be quite understandable yet be irreducible in the sense that no explication or analysis can render the poem's complexity of tone or complexity of emotion that, by dint of poetic art, has been hammered into the language.

When Perloff asserts that Ashbery's poetry is "irreducible" and that such irreducibility is the essence of the post-modernist lyric, she reduces the term "post-modernism" to a range of characteristics so narrow and oversimplified that it is no wonder she can find only one poet working in the mode. The true symptoms of the post-modernist poetic are, as one might expect, widespread; and, like the formal implications of Wordsworth's "Preface," they originate in a changing rhetorical contract between poet and reader. Less and less are poems offered as personal testimony whose prime test is sincerity and authenticity. Although such a contract, after the stultifying impersonality of late-modernism, once seemed to be a breath of fresh air, now it is seen to place too heavy a demand on a poet to scour his own experiences for authentic "material." Recoiling from the demands of testimony, yet still committed to poetry that treats of the self, a poet may now find himself resorting to forms that resemble extended hypotheses instead of testimony, poems that invite the reader to "suppose" and that then proceed to spin a mythology. As Hugo's "Degrees of Gray in Philipsburg" says, "You might come here Sunday on a whim./ Say your life broke down. . . ." Clearly the Hugo poem retains a strong testimonial flavor; but the grammar of hypothesis allows him to mythologize the landscape and the situation far more readily and extremely than if the poem had begun, "It's Sunday. I came here on a whim. My life broke down." The postmodernist mode, as it is woven through the diverse fabric of American poetry, finds its form, then, not through the cultivation of "discontinuity." Instead, through parody (of styles, of genres, of nonliterary forms) and through the nonassertive epistemology of its propositions, it strives to soften conventional distinctions between fiction and history and thereby to maximize the poet's freedom playfully to invent.